The Children's Book of THE COUNTRYSIDE

The material in this book is also available as three separate books: **Birdwatching, Trees and Leaves,** and **Wild Flowers,** in the Nature Trail series, published by Usborne Publishing.

Written by
Malcolm Hart, Ingrid Selberg
and Sue Tarsky

Consultant Editors
Peter Holden, Sally Heathcote,
Jean Mellanby, E. H. M. Harris

Designed by
Sally Burrough, Nick Eddison,
Mike Ricketts, Valerie Sargent.

Edited by
Sue Jacquemier

Illustrated by
Dave Ashby, John Barber,
David Baxter, Hilary Burn, Liz Butler,
Patrick Cox, John Francis, Victoria Gordon,
Tim Hayward, Christine Howes, Colin King,
Deborah King, Ken Lilly, Malcolm McGregor,
Richard Millington, David Nash,
Barbara Nicholson, Charles Pearson,
Gillian Platt, Valerie Sangster,
Gwen Simpson, George Thompson,
Joan Thompson, Joyce Tuhill

**Printed in Belgium by
Henri Proost, Turnhout,**

The Children's Book of THE COUNTRYSIDE

Contents

Mistle Thrush

Nuthatch

Siskin

Part 1 written by
Malcolm Hart

Consultant Editor
Peter Holden, National
Organizer of the Young
Ornithologists' Club

2

Part 1 BIRDS

This section tells you where to look for common European birds and how best to study them. It shows you some clues to look for, how birds live in different kinds of places, and how to collect information. Before you go out birdwatching, read the instructions and hints given in the first part of the section about what to take and what to wear. Remember to move very quietly so as not to disturb the birds, and never touch nests or eggs.

If you want to identify a bird, look first at the illustrations on pages 28–33, or look on the pages that deal with the kind of place where you saw the bird.

Once you can recognize common birds, you might like to study some of them in more detail. To help you to see them more often, try building a nesting box like the one shown on page 12, or make a bird garden (see page 10). These need not be expensive and you will be able to see plenty of birds that come to visit even when the weather is too bad to go out birdwatching.

Some of the birds in this book, and many others that can be seen, are now becoming rarer. This is mainly because their habitats are being destroyed —they often live only in very special kinds of places, like heaths or wetlands. They are also threatened by hunters and by pesticides, which kill off their food.

Stonechat

Bearded
Reedlings

How to be a Birdwatcher

The most important thing for any birdwatcher to have is a notebook. It is difficult to keep all the facts in your head and if you try you will probably forget some important points.

Try to keep any notes you make clear and readable. The picture shows how to set your notebook out. Try to draw the birds you see. Even a bad drawing is better than nothing.

When you get home, look up the bird you have seen in this book

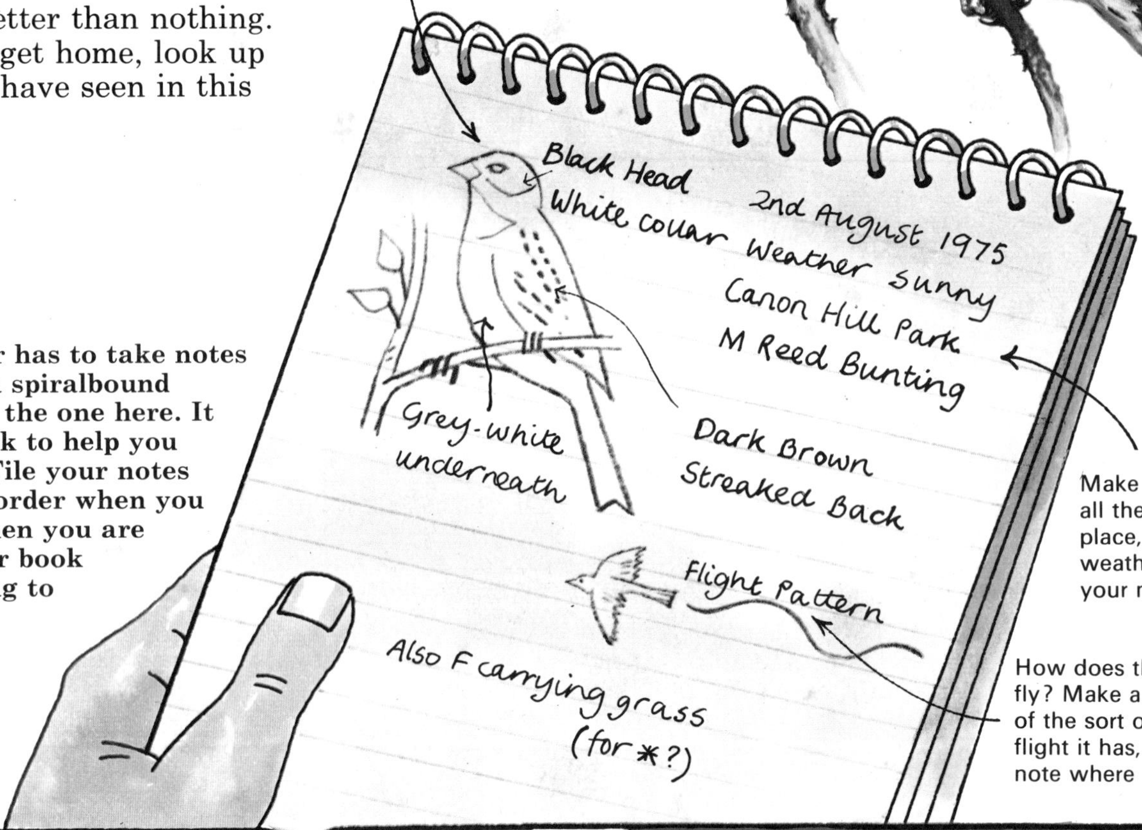

A birdwatcher has to take notes quickly. Use a spiralbound notebook like the one here. It has a stiff back to help you write easily. File your notes away in date order when you get home. When you are out, keep your book in a plastic bag to keep it dry.

Male Reed Bunting

Look for the shape and obvious marks first. The Reed Bunting has a sparrow-like body, a dark head, white collar and white outer tail feathers.

Black Head
White collar
2nd August 1975
Weather sunny
Canon Hill Park
M Reed Bunting
Grey-white underneath
Dark Brown Streaked Back
Flight Pattern
Also F carrying grass (for * ?)

Make sure you have all the details of place, date, and weather entered in your notebook.

How does the bird fly? Make a drawing of the sort of flight it has, and note where it goes.

Bird Shorthand

M = MALE
F = FEMALE
JUV = JUVENILE (YOUNG BIRD NOT IN ADULT FEATHERS)
* = NEST
C10 = ABOUT TEN (WHEN TALKING ABOUT NUMBERS OF BIRDS)

Use these signs instead of writing out the words—it will save you time. Take two pencils with you.

How to Stalk Birds

CAMOUFLAGE YOUR SHAPE BY STANDING IN FRONT OF OR BEHIND A TREE OR BUSH. YOUR DULL CLOTHES WILL BLEND IN WITH THE BACKGROUND. KEEP THE SUN BEHIND, SO THAT YOU ARE IN SHADOW AND THE BIRD IS IN SUNLIGHT

IF THERE IS NO COVER, CRAWL CLOSER USING YOUR ELBOWS AND FEET. DON'T WEAR CLOTHES THAT RUSTLE WHEN YOU MOVE. NEVER MAKE QUICK MOVEMENTS IN THE OPEN

What to Wear

Travel as light as possible

Hat or hood (remember to wear dull colours)

Binoculars

Anorak or warm coat

Notebook and pencils

One or two pairs of socks

Trousers tucked into wellingtons

Buying Binoculars

The best size to get is 7×50 or 8×30

Choose the lightest pair you can find

Binoculars are not essential for the beginner, but if you want some, go to a shop with someone who knows about binoculars, and try several pairs to see how they feel.

HOWEVER LIGHT YOUR BINOCULARS ARE, THEY WILL START TO FEEL HEAVY AFTER A WHILE. TO TAKE THE WEIGHT OFF YOUR NECK, TIE SOME STRING ONTO THE STRAP AS SHOWN

Binocular strap

String tied to strap and belt

Belt

Quick Field Sketches

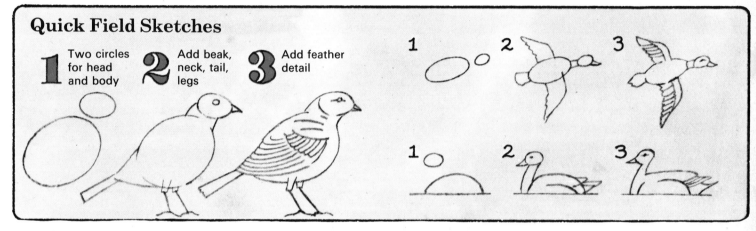

1 Two circles for head and body

2 Add beak, neck, tail, legs

3 Add feather detail

1   2   3

1   2   3

The best way to take notes on the birds you see is to draw quick sketches of them. Begin by drawing two circles—one for the body and one for the head. Notice the size and position of the head and body before you start. Then add the tail, beak and legs. Fill in the details of the feathers if you have time. Practise drawing the birds you can see from your window first.

IF YOU GO TO THE SAME PLACE OFTEN, PUT UP A LITTLE SCREEN OF BRANCHES THEN YOU CAN MOVE ABOUT WITHOUT FRIGHTENING THE BIRDS

TRY TO APPROACH DOWNWIND OF THE BIRD— THAT IS, WITH THE WIND BLOWING IN YOUR FACE. THEN SOUND WILL NOT CARRY SO EASILY TO THE BIRD

WIND

RUSTLE

CLOMP

WRONG! THIS BIRDWATCHER WILL NOT GET FAR. HE IS LOADED DOWN WITH HEAVY EQUIPMENT AND CANNOT MOVE EASILY AND QUIETLY. THE BIRDS CAN SEE HIS HUMAN SHAPE SILHOUETTED AGAINST THE SKY SO THEY FLY OFF

What to Look for

These pages tell you what to look for when you want to identify a bird. When you see a bird for the first time, there are several questions you should ask. What size is it? Compare it with a bird you know like a Sparrow or a Blackbird.

Has it any obvious marks like the Reed Bunting's black head and white outer tail feathers? How does it fly and feed? How does it behave? Where is it? What colour is it? Some differences in colour can be confusing: there are some examples opposite.

A female Sparrowhawk chasing a male Reed Bunting. The labels give examples of the kind of things to note down when you see a bird.

Rounded wings

Black head

White collar

Hooked beak

White outer tail feathers

Long tail feathers

Yellow legs

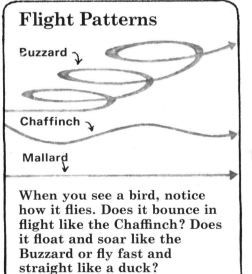

Flight Patterns

Buzzard

Chaffinch

Mallard

When you see a bird, notice how it flies. Does it bounce in flight like the Chaffinch? Does it float and soar like the Buzzard or fly fast and straight like a duck?

Shapes in Flight

Tern

Heron

Crow

Goose

Curlew

Magpie

Woodpecker

What sort of shape does the bird make when it is flying? Has it a long or short neck or tail? Has it got short rounded wings or long narrow ones? Do its feet stick out behind its tail?

Sex Differences

Male

Female

Blackbirds

The males of some birds, like the Blackbird, have different coloured feathers and beaks from the females.

Colour Changes

Summer

Winter

Black-Headed Gulls

Some birds, like the Black-Headed Gull, have a different plumage in winter from the one they have in summer.

Age Differences

Adult

Juvenile (Young)

Robins

In some birds, like the Robin, the young look very different from their parents.

Looking at Beaks

Curlew

Carrion Crow

Greenfinch

Heron

Beaks can give you clues to what a bird eats. The Crow's beak is a general-purpose tool. The Greenfinch's beak is more suited to eating seeds. The Curlew uses its long beak for probing for food in mud and the Heron uses its beak for catching fish.

ONE WAY TO IDENTIFY A BIRD IS FROM ITS SONG. GO OUT WITH SOMEONE WHO KNOWS BIRD SONG WELL, OR BORROW RECORDS OF BIRD SONG FROM YOUR LOCAL LIBRARY

Watch What Birds are Doing

Grey Wagtail

Treecreeper

Turnstone

The Wagtail often patrols in mud or short grass. It wags its tail up and down. Sometimes it makes a dash after an insect.

The treecreeper creeps around tree trunks, picking out insects from the bark with its thin, curved bill.

The turnstone walks along the beach turning over seaweed and stones, looking for small creatures to eat.

Clues and Tracks

Sometimes you can tell which birds have been in an area by the clues that they leave behind. After some practice these are easy to recognize. Their feathers and the remains of meals are the ones you will see most often.

You may not be able to identify the feathers you find straight away. But later you may find a dead bird or see a bird in a zoo or museum that has feathers like the ones you have collected. Remember that most birds have feathers of many different colours and sizes.

Jay feather

Magpie feather

Egg of a **Sandwich Tern** eaten by a **Gull**

Oystercatcher skull

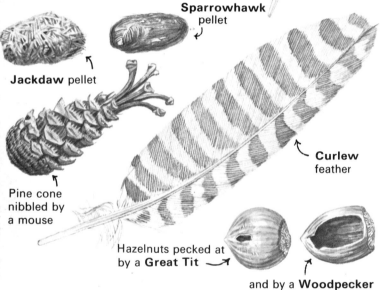

Jackdaw pellet

Sparrowhawk pellet

Pine cone nibbled by a mouse

Curlew feather

Hazelnuts pecked at by a **Great Tit**

and by a **Woodpecker**

ALWAYS MAKE SURE YOU HAVE SOMEWHERE TO KEEP THE THINGS THAT YOU COLLECT. LABEL EVERYTHING CAREFULLY AND IN DETAIL ~ THE MORE INFORMATION THE BETTER. ALWAYS WASH YOUR HANDS AFTER TOUCHING THINGS YOU HAVE COLLECTED

If you find the remains of nuts and pinecones, be careful how you identify the creatures that have been eating them, as these things are the food of squirrels and mice, as well as of birds.

Collecting Feathers and Wings

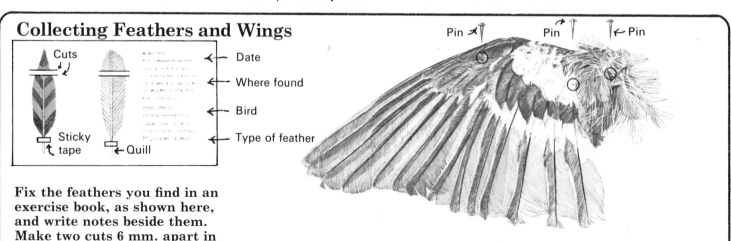

Cuts

Sticky tape

Quill

Date

Where found

Bird

Type of feather

Pin

Pin

Pin

Fix the feathers you find in an exercise book, as shown here, and write notes beside them. Make two cuts 6 mm. apart in the page. Thread the feather through and stick the quill down with tape.

Wings cut from dead birds can be dried and kept. Pin the wing out on a piece of stiff board. It

should dry in a few days and can then be placed in an envelope with a label and some mothballs.

Pinecones

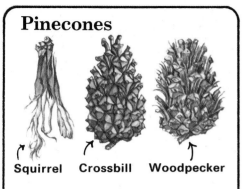

Squirrel   Crossbill   Woodpecker

Here are three examples of pinecones that have been attacked by birds or animals. They break open the cones in different ways to search for seeds.

Nuts

Nuthatch (Hazelnut)   Hawfinch (Cherry)

Woodmouse (Hazelnut)   Great Tit (Walnut)

Animals all have their own ways of opening nuts. Mice chew neat little holes while birds leave jagged holes or split the nuts in half.

The Thrush's Anvil

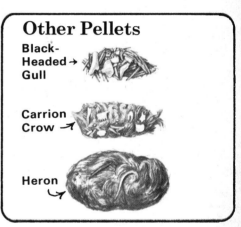

Snail shell   Anvil   Broken shells

Song Thrushes use stones to break open snail shells. Look for the thrush's "anvil"—it will be surrounded by the remains of the bird's meal.

Owl Pellets

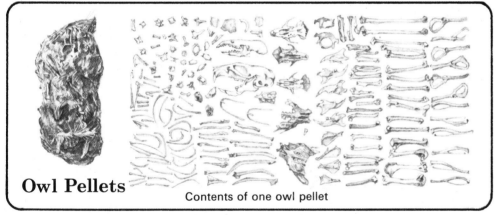

Contents of one owl pellet

Other Pellets

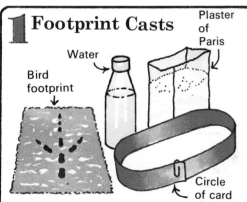

Black-Headed Gull

Carrion Crow

Heron

Owls swallow small animals and birds whole, and then cough up the fur, feathers and bones as a pellet. You can find these beneath trees or posts where the owl rests. Pull a pellet apart and sort out the bones. The easiest to identify are the skulls of animals which the owl has eaten.

Many birds other than owls produce pellets. But it is harder to identify what is in them as most other birds do not eat large enough animals.

1 Footprint Casts

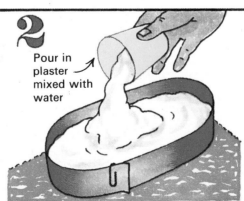

Plaster of Paris

Water

Bird footprint

Circle of card

To make plaster casts you will need water, plaster of Paris, a beaker and a strip of card bent into a circle, and held by a paperclip.

2

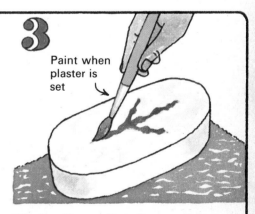

Pour in plaster mixed with water

Put the card around the footprint. Mix the plaster, pour it into the circle and let it harden. Wrap the cast in tissues and take it home.

3

Paint when plaster is set

Wash off any dirt. Leave the cast for a few days and then carefully remove it from the card. Paint the footprint and then varnish it.

Making a Bird Garden

This picture shows many of the birds that visit gardens or window-sills for food. Different kinds of food attract different birds. Put out bones, suet, cheese, oats, peanuts, sunflower seeds, currants and bits of bacon rind. Scatter food in the open for birds that prefer to eat on the ground, and build a bird bath.

Key to Birds

1	Greenfinch	8	Chaffinch
2	House Sparrow	9	Blackbird
3	Blue Tit	10	Mistle Thrush
4	Great Tit	11	Goldfinch
5	Robin	12	Song Thrush
6	Coal Tit	13	Dunnock
7	Starling	14	Bullfinch

REMEMBER:- DON'T ATTRACT BIRDS TO A SPOT WHERE YOU KNOW CATS ARE LURKING. DON'T STOP FEEDING BIRDS SUDDENLY IN WINTER—THEY RELY ON YOUR FOOD SUPPLY AND MAY STARVE IF THEY CANNOT FIND FOOD ELSEWHERE

Feeding Chart

	CHEESE	BACON	NUTS
BLUE TIT	✓	✓✓✓	✓✓✓✓
ROBIN			
STARLING			
BLACKBIRD			

Make a chart of the kinds of food you see different birds eating. Which birds like nuts best? Tick the boxes each time you see the bird eat something.

Plants That Birds Like to Eat

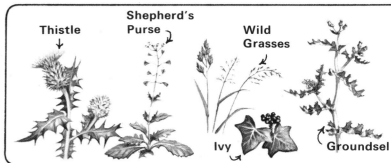

Thistle

Shepherd's Purse

Wild Grasses

Ivy

Groundsel

All these plants are good bird food. If you have a garden try to let a little patch grow wild. Weeds like Thistles, Groundsel and Shepherd's Purse have seeds that birds like

to eat. Trees and bushes like Hawthorn, Cotoneaster, Rowan and Elder have lots of good berries in the autumn. Some birds like over-ripe apples and sultanas. Dig

Putting out Food

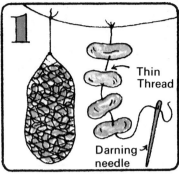

Thin Thread

Darning needle

Supermarkets often sell vegetables in nets. Fill one of these with unsalted peanuts, or thread peanuts on a string, and hang them up.

Matchstick

Darning needle

Melt the fat in a warm oven

Yoghurt pot

To make a feeding bell with a yoghurt pot, fill the pot with a mixture of breadcrumbs, currants, cooked (not raw) potato and oatmeal. Pour on

some melted fat and wait until it hardens before you hang the feeder up. Tits and Finches will be able to cling on and feed.

Make a Bird Table

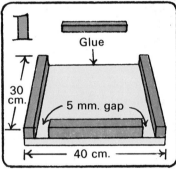

Glue

30 cm.

5 mm. gap

40 cm.

You will need a piece of outdoor quality plywood about 40 cm. × 30 cm., and four strips of dowel, each about 30 cm. long. Glue the dowel to the plywood.

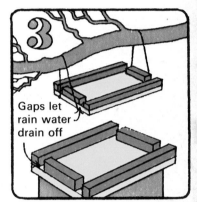

3 cm. screws

Put screws in under dowel strips

When the glue has dried, turn the table over and put in two screws on every side as shown. Protect your table with a wood preservative and screw it to a box or tub.

Gaps let rain water drain off

To make a hanging table, put four screw-eyes into the sides and hang it from a branch. Clean the table regularly with disinfectant.

Make a Bird Bath

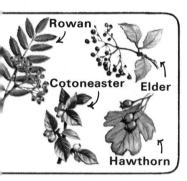

Rowan

Cotoneaster   Elder

Hawthorn

over a patch of earth to make it easier for Blackbirds and Thrushes to find worms and insects.

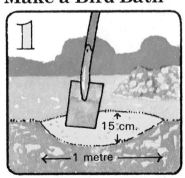

15 cm.

1 metre

Choose a place not too close to the feeding area. Dig a hole with sloping sides about 15 cm. deep and one metre wide. Dig from the middle outwards.

Make sure polythene has no tears

Line the hole with a piece of strong polythene (a dustbin liner will do). Weight the plastic down with stones and sprinkle gravel or sand over the lining.

Put a few stones and a short branch in the middle of the bath to make a perch. Fill the bath with water. Keep it full (and ice-free in winter).

Making a Nesting Box

You can encourage birds to come to your garden in spring by building them a nesting box. If the entrance hole is small a Blue Tit is the bird most likely to nest in the box. If it is larger you may find a House Sparrow using it. Other birds, like Great Tits, Starlings, Tree Sparrows, Nuthatches and even Wrens sometimes use nesting boxes. You can look inside your box but try not to disturb the birds. You can always watch them from indoors.

TO MAKE YOUR NESTING BOX YOU WILL NEED SOME PLYWOOD THAT IS 12 MM THICK. EITHER GET THE WOOD CUT TO SIZE AT THE SHOP OR ASK AN ADULT TO SAW IT FOR YOU

How to Cut the Wood

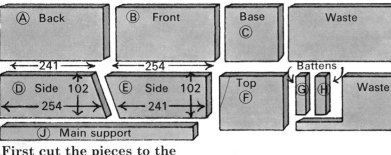

Ⓐ Back   Ⓑ Front   Base Ⓒ   Waste
←241→   ←254→
Ⓓ Side 102   Ⓔ Side 102   Top Ⓕ   Battens Ⓖ Ⓗ   Waste
←254→   ←241→
Ⓙ Main support

First cut the pieces to the following sizes:

A 254 mm. × 127 mm.
B 241 mm. × 127 mm.
C 127 mm. × 127 mm.
D 241 mm. × 102 mm.
E 254 mm. × 102 mm.
F 152 mm. × 127 mm.
G 102 mm. × 25 mm.
H 102 mm. × 25 mm.
J 510 mm. × 25 mm.

Overall length: 915 mm.
Overall width: 254 mm.

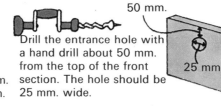

50 mm.

Drill the entrance hole with a hand drill about 50 mm. from the top of the front section. The hole should be 25 mm. wide.

25 mm.

Side Ⓔ removed to show how box is made

Ⓕ Ⓗ Ⓖ Ⓐ Ⓑ Ⓒ

1

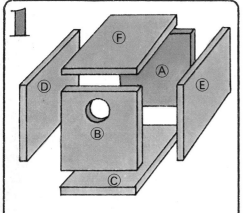

First arrange all the pieces to make sure that they fit together properly. Then drill holes for all the screws.

2

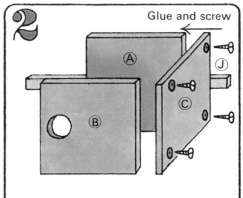

Glue and screw

Fix the main support onto the back with two screws. Glue and screw the bottom onto the back and then the front.

3

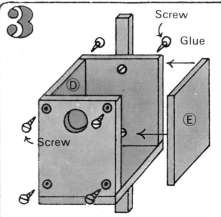

Screw   Glue   Screw

Glue and then fit the side pieces into place. Screw them on if they fit properly.

Where to Put the Box

Your completed box should be fixed to a tree or to an ivy-covered wall. The entrance hole should not face south or west as the heat from direct sunlight might kill the young birds. Fix it about two metres above the ground (away from cats). Empty out the old nest every winter, disinfect the box and give it a new coat of wood preservative before replacing it.

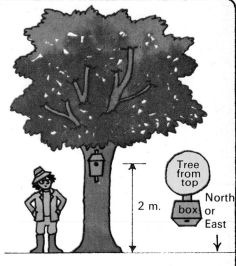

2 m.

Tree from top

box

North or East ↓

Keeping a Record

Try to make a note of what happens in your nesting box. You may even see some birds visiting the box in winter. They use boxes to sleep in. The notes below tell you the sort of thing to record.

1 Date of first visit.
2 Number of birds visiting.
3 Date bird first enters box.
4 Dates birds bring nest material.
5 Type of nest material.
6 Date birds first bring food.
7 Type of food.
8 Date young leave nest.

Other Types of Box

Special nesting boxes can be bought for House Martins. You can fix them under the edge of the roof.

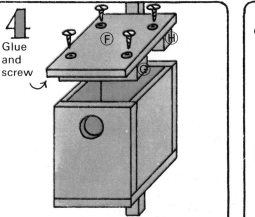

4
Glue and screw
(F) (H) (G)

Screw the two short battens onto the top piece. Make sure the removable lid fits tightly.

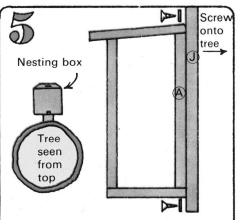

5
Nesting box
Tree seen from top
Screw onto tree →
(J) (A) (I)

Paint the outside of the box with wood preservative and let it dry. Screw or nail it on to a tree (see above).

Side removed to show how box is made

165 mm.

An open-fronted box can be made for other birds. It is like the nesting box shown opposite but the front panel is only 165 mm. high.

13

The Nesting Season

The nesting season is a time of great activity for all birds. First they have to find a place where they can build their nests and feed. This area then becomes their territory. When they have found a mate they have to build a nest, lay eggs and rear their young. With all this going on, it is not difficult to find out when and where a bird is building its nest or feeding its young. A bird carrying something in its beak is the most common sign. On these pages are some clues to help you.

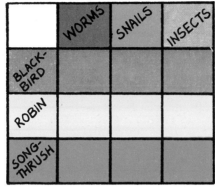

Food Chart
Make a food chart to record which birds you see carrying

	WORMS	SNAILS	INSECTS
BLACK-BIRD			
ROBIN			
SONG-THRUSH			

food to their young, and the type of food.

The Song Thrush builds its nest in a bush. There are usually four or five eggs. Both parents feed the young birds with worms and snails.

REMEMBER~IT IS AGAINST THE LAW TO DISTURB BREEDING BIRDS OR THEIR NESTS AND EGGS. BUT IF YOU ARE CAREFUL YOU CAN WATCH FROM A DISTANCE WITHOUT UPSETTING THEM AT ALL

The adult bird arrives at the nest with food. It pushes the food into the mouth of one of the young birds, removes any droppings from the nest and flies off to collect more food.

When a parent bird approaches the nest, the young birds beg for food with wide, open mouths.

Spotting Nesting Birds

Rook

Nightingale

Stonechat

Droppings

In the spring you will often see birds carrying nest material in their beaks. Rooks break off large twigs from trees for their nests.

Look out and listen for a bird singing in the same place every day during spring and summer. It is probably a sign that it is breeding.

You may see adult birds carrying droppings away from the nest in their beaks. They do this to keep the nest clean.

Nest Materials

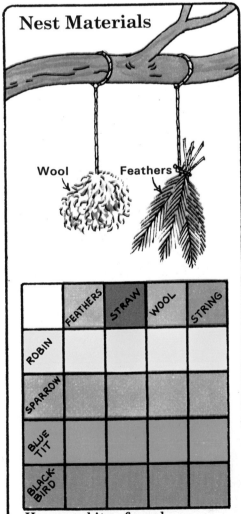

Wool   Feathers

	FEATHERS	STRAW	WOOL	STRING
ROBIN				
SPARROW				
BLUE TIT				
BLACK-BIRD				

Hang up bits of wool, feathers, straw and string from a tree. Make a note of what different materials birds collect to use for their nests.

Where Birds Nest

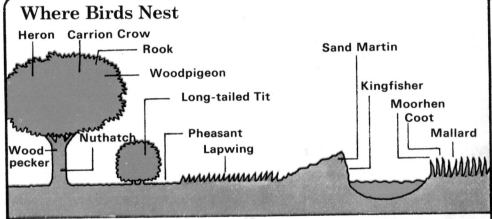

Heron Carrion Crow
Rook
Woodpigeon
Long-tailed Tit
Sand Martin
Kingfisher
Moorhen
Coot
Mallard
Nuthatch
Pheasant
Lapwing
Wood-pecker

In the country, birds nest in many different places. They use trees and hedges, the shelter of steep banks and holes in trees. Some birds, like the Lapwing, make hardly any nest at all. They lay their eggs in a shallow hole in the ground.

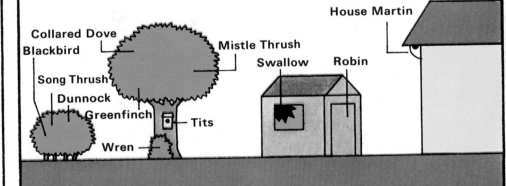

Collared Dove
Blackbird
Mistle Thrush
House Martin
Song Thrush
Swallow Robin
Dunnock
Greenfinch
Tits
Wren

Many birds nest in gardens but only in sheltered places, safe from cats and dogs. They use thick bushes, trees, ivy-covered walls and sheds as well as nesting boxes. Some birds, like the House Martin, even build under the roof.

Ponds and Inland Waterways

Ducks are the birds you are most likely to see on a pond. They have quite long necks, webbed feet and wide, flat bills. They are all good swimmers. Most of them feed on the water weeds and plant life in the pond. There are three kinds of duck—the diving ducks, like the Tufted Duck, the dabblers, like the Mallard, that often up-end for their food and the rarer fish-eating ducks called Sawbills. Look out for other water birds like Swans, Geese, Moorhens and Coots.

Mallards are probably the commonest birds on the pond. The females (ducks) are much less colourful than the males. The correct word for a male duck is "drake".

Young Mallards

Male Mallard

Female Mallard

It uses its long, flat bill to sift the water for food.

Both male and female ducks have a blue flash on each wing called a speculum.

How Water Birds Feed

Swallow catching insects over the water

Pintail up-ending

Kingfisher diving for fish

Tufted Duck diving

Wigeon grazing on land

Moorhen feeding in reeds by the water

Heron fishing on the edge of the pond

Mallard dabbling on the surface

Mute Swan fishing with head and neck under water

Watch how the birds feed on your local pond. Which birds up-end the most? Which dive most often?

Why do you think some birds feed differently from others?

Taking-Off and Landing

Goldeneye

Most water birds are heavy, and have to work hard to get airborne. Many of them run over the surface, flapping their wings until they get up enough speed to take off. To land, they fly low over the water, with their feet sticking out to act as a brake.

Swimming

Shoveler

Coot

Moorhen

Webbed feet are the best feet for swimming. The web opens to push hard against the water, like a frogman's flipper. When the foot comes back, the web closes so that the foot does not drag through the water. Coots spend a lot of time on land. They have partly webbed feet. Moorhens have hardly any webbing. They jerk their heads backwards and forwards when swimming.

Moulting

Female Mallard

Male Mallard

Ducks moult in late summer. The drake loses his colourful feathers and for a time looks rather like the female. New feathers have grown by early winter.

Chicks

Mallard

Young Mallards

Gull

Mallard

Great Crested Grebe

New chicks are taken to the water by their mother. The chicks fall in and can swim straight away.

When danger threatens Mallard chicks, the duck stretches out her neck and quacks loudly. The chicks dive to escape.

Great Crested Grebes are fish-eating water birds. The male and female both look after the young and carry their chicks on their backs.

Woodlands and Forests

All types of woods are good places for birds but you will see the bird most easily in places that are not too dark. Woods with open spaces or pools have more plants and insects for the birds to feed on.

The **Goldcrest** (9 cm) is the smallest European bird. It is often found in coniferous or mixed woods.

The **Black Woodpecker** (46 cm) is the largest European Woodpecker. It is not found in Britain but breeds in other parts of Europe, mainly in coniferous forests.

The **Chiffchaff** (11 cm) is smaller than a Sparrow and is a summer migrant from Africa. It is often found in deciduous woods and in young pine plantations.

CONIFEROUS FORESTS

BROADLEAVED WOODS

The **Coal Tit** (11.5 cm) is only a little larger than a Goldcrest. It nests in coniferous forests.

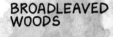

The **Green Woodpecker** (32 cm) is the same size as a domestic pigeon. It is frequently seen on the ground, feeding on ants, and is usually found in deciduous woods.

The **Nightingale** (16.5 cm) can often be heard singing in woods and forests but is rarely seen. It builds its nest among trees and bushes close to the ground.

The **Chaffinch** (15 cm) is a common bird, often found in broad-leaved woodlands and coniferous woods. In winter it prefers open land.

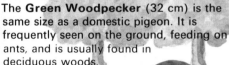

The **Woodcock** (34 cm) is found in deciduous woods where its plumage blends in perfectly with the dead leaves on the ground.

The **Lesser Spotted Woodpecker** (14.5 cm) is the smallest European Woodpecker. It is found in deciduous woods.

The **Nuthatch** (14 cm) feeds on nuts from hazel, beech and oak trees.

Woods with broad-leaved trees such as oak and beech contain many more birds than old pine forests or other coniferous forests. Young pine plantations and mixed woods which have many different kinds of trees in them, also have lots of birds.

The sizes given are beak-to-tail measurements.

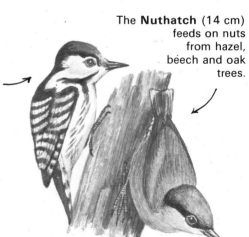

Food of Woodland Birds

IF IT IS WINDY, WATCH OUT FOR FALLING BRANCHES IN THE WOODS. TRY NOT TO STAND OR SIT NEAR TREES WHICH HAVE NESTS IN THEM. YOU MIGHT FRIGHTEN AWAY THE PARENT BIRDS

In autumn **Jays** collect the acorns from oak trees. They bury many of them and dig them up when they are short of food.

The **Tawny Owl** feeds on small animals like mice. It has very good eyesight and hearing and can catch its food even on the darkest nights.

Many birds, like the **Garden Warbler,** feed on caterpillars which are very common in woods.

The **Pied Flycatcher** catches insects by swooping down on them in a short flight from a lookout branch.

Holes in Trees

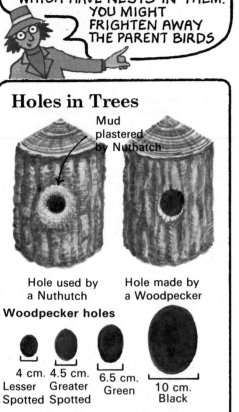

Mud plastered by Nuthatch

Hole used by a Nuthutch | Hole made by a Woodpecker

Woodpecker holes

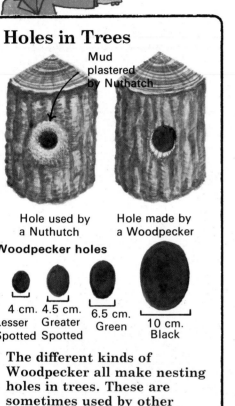

| 4 cm. Lesser Spotted | 4.5 cm. Greater Spotted | 6.5 cm. Green | 10 cm. Black |

The different kinds of Woodpecker all make nesting holes in trees. These are sometimes used by other birds like the Nuthatch, or animals like bats and dormice.

Special Beaks

Hawfinch   Crossbill

Some birds like the Hawfinch and the Crossbill have special beaks for eating seeds.

Woodlands at Night

Many different kinds of owl live in woods. They range in size from the Pygmy Owl which is only 16.5 cm. high, to the Eagle Owl, which can be as large as 71 cm.

These three owls are all drawn to the same scale

These four owls are all drawn to the same scale

Pygmy Owl

Scops Owl

Little Owl

Little Owl

Long-eared Owl

Tawny Owl

Eagle Owl

Nightjar

The Nightjar sleeps during the day, so is rarely seen. Its song can be heard after dark in summer.

Towns and Cities

You do not have to live in the country to be a birdwatcher. In the middle of towns you may only find Pigeons, Starlings and House Sparrows but where there are gardens and parks you will see many other kinds of birds. Some of these birds are quite used to people and can be very tame. This means that you will probably be able to get quite close to them and see them very clearly. The illustrations show some of the more common birds you might see in towns and cities.

The **Kestrel** is a town as well as a country bird. But the town Kestrel usually feeds on Sparrows instead of mice and beetles, and nests on high buildings instead of in trees.

1 Cliff Birds that Live in Towns

Black Redstart

Black Redstarts once nested on sea-cliffs and rocks. Now you are more likely to find them in towns. They build their nests on buildings.

The **Long-tailed Tit** is a hedge bird that can often be seen in parks and gardens. In autumn and winter family groups of about a dozen gather together.

The **Black-headed Gull** is one of the commonest town gulls. You will often see large numbers of them near reservoirs and gravel pits.

You will sometimes hear the warbling song of the **Skylark** as it flies high above parks and wasteland. In winter you may see flocks around gravel pits and sewage works.

You will hardly ever see a **Swift** on the ground. It feeds and even sleeps as it is flying. At dusk you may see flocks of Swifts circling high above the roof-tops.

Cities are surprisingly good places to look for birds. All birds need food and places to nest and sleep. Most gardens (3) and parks (2) have some trees and bushes where birds can nest and sleep without being disturbed by people. Many birds find perching places on buildings (5). Gulls fly out to sleep at gravel pits (1) or reservoirs (4) at night. Everywhere people spill or leave food on which birds can live. On the edge of cities birds find lots of food at sewage works (4), rubbish dumps(1). Railway

2

Rock Dove

Pigeons

The Pigeon is a relation of the Rock Dove, which nests on sea-cliffs. But the town Pigeon is now much more common than the Rock Dove and is often very tame. It feeds on bread and any other scraps it finds in parks or in the streets.

Noisy City Birds

Starling

Starlings are one of the commonest city birds and are usually found in huge, noisy flocks. In summer many of them move to the country.

House Martins build their mud nests under the roofs of many town houses.

Carrion Crows are quite common in parks and gardens.

Magpies are large black and white birds and are common in parks and gardens. They use twigs to build their nests in trees and tall hedges.

Swallows look rather like House Martins but have longer tail feathers. You can often see them catching flies over rivers, gravel pits and sewage works.

sidings and canals (6) where food is unloaded and often spilt are also good places for birds to find food, and have fewer people to disturb them. Many birds eat the seeds of weeds growing on waste ground and building sites. In winter, when there is little food in the countryside, many birds fly to the cities. There people put out food for them in parks and gardens.

Sea Coasts

The coast is always a good place for birds. In summer many birds fly to Europe from Africa and the Antarctic. They come to the shore to breed. In winter, small wading birds like the Knot come from the north to feed and wait for spring. Most of the cliff-nesting birds spend the winter far out at sea. Unfortunately, every year many birds lose their eggs and babies because people tread on the nests or stop the parent birds from feeding their young by frightening them away.

Waders' Beaks

Birds can find a lot of food on the beach. The shape of a wading bird's beak depends on the sort of food it eats. You can try to find out what the birds are eating by digging up the sand and looking for the food in it.

Avocet sifts for food

Curlew probes deeply

Dunlin picks food on and under the surface

Oystercatcher feeds on shellfish.

The Brent Goose is a rare winter visitor from Greenland or northern Russia where it breeds. It feeds on a plant called eelgrass which grows only on mudflats. It is the smallest wild goose.

Brent Goose

Shelduck

Shelduck

The Shelduck is one of the commonest large birds you will see on a salt marsh. It sometimes builds its nest in an old rabbit burrow.

Knot (summer plumage)

In winter large flocks of Knot fly south from their northern breeding grounds. They feed on sandy or muddy shores.

Common Tern

The Tern breeds on salt marshes, shingle or sandy shores. It builds its nest in a hollow in the ground.

Salt Marsh

Sandy Shore

Shingle Beach

Fish-Eaters' Beaks

Fish-eating birds do not all have the same kind of beak. The shape of the beak depends on the size and type of fish that the bird eats.

Common Tern

Razorbill

Gannet

Nesting Places

In winter cliffs are almost deserted but during the breeding season they are like large bird cities. The whole cliff is used for nesting. Each type of bird has its favourite spot for nesting.

Puffins dig nesting burrows in the soil on the cliff-top. They use their huge, brightly coloured bills for digging and push away the soil with their webbed feet.

Puffin

The cliff-top is also the Gannet's favourite nesting place. Gannets nest in large numbers and build their untidy nests only about one metre apart from each other.

Gannet

The Fulmar is a large silver-grey bird that spends most of its time out at sea. It looks rather like a gull but holds its wings straighter and stiffer when it is flying. It nests on rock ledges and sometimes on window ledges.

Razorbill

The Razorbill lays its one egg in cracks in the cliff or under rocks. The nest is sometimes a few pieces of seaweed but there is usually no proper nest at all.

Guillemot

Like the Razorbill, the Guillemot makes no nest. It lays a single pear-shaped egg on a rock ledge. The shape of the egg helps to stop it rolling off. Guillemots nest in large numbers, crowded very close together.

Fulmar

The Cormorant's feathers are not waterproof, so when it leaves the water it often stands on a rock or post holding out its wings to dry. It builds a large untidy nest of seaweed and sticks in which it lays three or four eggs.

WATCH THE BIRDS AND TRY TO SEE WHAT THEY EAT. HOW DO THEY USE THEIR BEAKS WHEN FEEDING? HAVE THEY ANY SPECIAL WAY OF GETTING THEIR FOOD?

The Shag and the Cormorant are quite difficult to tell apart. The Shag is the smaller of the two and does not have the Cormorant's white face. In the breeding season it grows a little curly crest.

Cormorant

Shag

Cliffs

Mountains and Moorlands

Many of the birds that live on mountains and moorlands are well known because they are game-birds like the Grouse, or large and powerful birds of prey like the Buzzard or Golden Eagle. But you will see fewer birds here than by the coast or in woods because there is less food for them to eat. The smaller birds eat bilberries, the young shoots of heather and the seeds from mosses and grasses. The larger birds of prey feed mainly on small birds and animals.

The **Golden Eagle** is the largest bird that is found on moors and mountains. It is very rare in most parts of Europe.

The **Buzzard** is one of the commonest of the large birds of prey. It is similar to the Golden Eagle but is smaller and stubbier.

The **Short-eared Owl** nests on the ground. It often hunts in the daytime and feeds on small animals like voles and lemmings.

The **Raven** is the largest of the Crow family. It is even larger than the Buzzard. It flies slowly but powerfully and sometimes tumbles through the air.

The **Meadow Pipit** is the commonest small bird that you will see on moorland. It feeds on insects.

These two birds look different but are in fact very closely related. **The Red Grouse** is only found in Britain and the **Willow Grouse** only in Europe. The Willow Grouse is shown here in its partial winter plumage.

Willow Grouse

Red Grouse

Short-tailed Vole

24

EVERY YEAR PEOPLE GET LOST ON MOUNTAINS OR MOORS. MAKE SURE IT IS NOT YOU. NEVER GO ON YOUR OWN AND ALWAYS TELL SOMEONE WHERE YOU ARE GOING. KEEP TO PATHS AND WEAR WARM CLOTHES. MOUNTAINS CAN BE COLD EVEN IN SUMMER

An Underwater Fisher

The Dipper lives by fast-flowing mountain streams. It feeds on insects that it catches under the water.

Dipper

Shrikes

Shrikes (or Butcher Birds) have a habit of pinning their spare food such as bees, beetles and even small birds, onto branches or barbed wire. When food is scarce they may go back to collect it. The Redbacked Shrike is a rather rare summer visitor. The Great Grey Shrike breeds in Northern Europe and flies south in the winter.

Redbacked Shrike

Beetle

Great Grey Shrike

Changing Colour with the Seasons

Ptarmigan in summer

Ptarmigan in winter

The Ptarmigan can hide from its enemies because it always looks the same colour as the countryside. In summer its coat is mainly brown but in winter it turns pure white. It lives in the mountains of northern Europe.

The **Golden Plover** usually breeds on moors and hills. It lays its four eggs in a nest on the ground.

The **Wheatear** builds its nest in holes in walls and in old rabbit burrows.

The **Black Grouse** lives on the borders of moorland. The male (Blackcock) has a lyre-shaped tail.

The **Ring Ouzel** is a relative of the Blackbird and lives in remote mountain valleys.

Lemming (not found in Britain)

Migrating Birds

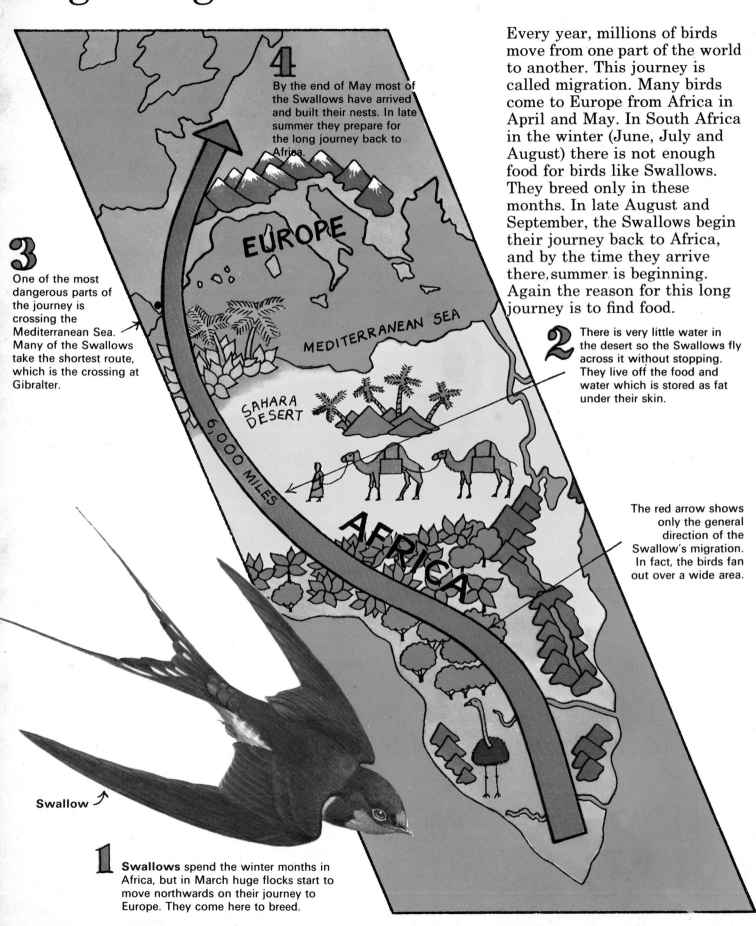

4 By the end of May most of the Swallows have arrived and built their nests. In late summer they prepare for the long journey back to Africa.

3 One of the most dangerous parts of the journey is crossing the Mediterranean Sea. Many of the Swallows take the shortest route, which is the crossing at Gibralter.

EUROPE

MEDITERRANEAN SEA

6,000 MILES

SAHARA DESERT

AFRICA

Swallow ↗

1 **Swallows** spend the winter months in Africa, but in March huge flocks start to move northwards on their journey to Europe. They come here to breed.

Every year, millions of birds move from one part of the world to another. This journey is called migration. Many birds come to Europe from Africa in April and May. In South Africa in the winter (June, July and August) there is not enough food for birds like Swallows. They breed only in these months. In late August and September, the Swallows begin their journey back to Africa, and by the time they arrive there, summer is beginning. Again the reason for this long journey is to find food.

2 There is very little water in the desert so the Swallows fly across it without stopping. They live off the food and water which is stored as fat under their skin.

The red arrow shows only the general direction of the Swallow's migration. In fact, the birds fan out over a wide area.

White Stork

Redwing

TRY TO KEEP A NOTE OF THE FIRST AND LAST DATES ON WHICH YOU SEE MIGRANT BIRDS. KEEP A RECORD OF THE WEATHER IN YOUR AREA DURING SPRING AND AUTUMN AND SEE IF THIS AFFECTS THE DATES ON WHICH BIRDS ARRIVE OR LEAVE

In some areas of Europe, flocks of large birds like the White Stork can be seen waiting by the coast. When the weather is good enough, they cross the sea and continue their migration.

The Redwing is a member of the Thrush family. In winter it flies south through Europe travelling mainly at night in large flocks.

Summer Visitors

Blackcap

Willow Warbler

These warblers are two of the commonest small birds that visit Europe in the summer. They come from Africa but in some winters a few Blackcaps stay in Europe.

Hoopoe

The Hoopoe, with its floppy flight, does not seem capable of flying far, but every autumn it flies to Africa and returns in spring.

Arctic Tern

Some birds fly even longer distances than the Swallow. One of these is the Arctic Tern. It flies from the Arctic, where it breeds, all the way to the southern tip of South America or South Africa. During the journey it stays mostly out at sea.

Arctic Circle

Routes taken by Arctic Terns

Arctic Tern

Starling

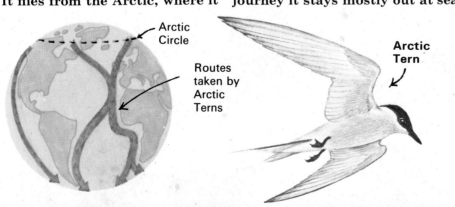

Many Starlings fly south in winter and are attracted to bright lights, such as lighthouses, at night. Many of them are killed by flying into buildings where they see lights.

Common Birds to Spot

Sparrow-sized Birds

The notes under each bird give its size from beak to tail. Each panel contains birds of a similar size. The coloured dots beside each bird tell you where to look for it and the red arrows show the points to look for.

- ● Water
- ● Woods
- ● Towns and Gardens
- ● Fields

The birds inside this panel are all drawn to the same scale.

Wren. 9.5 cm. Smallest bird you will see in gardens. Holds its tail cocked over its back.

Goldcrest. 9 cm. Smallest European bird. Feeds on insects and spiders.

Blue Tit. 11.5 cm. Only tit with blue head and wings. One of the most common garden birds.

Treecreeper. 12.5 cm. This mouse-like bird climbs trees.

Nuthatch. 14 cm. Has a long straight bill used for cracking open nuts.

Long-tailed Tit. 14 cm. Tail very long. Often seen in small flocks.

Great Tit. 14 cm. Has a black band down its belly.

Coal Tit. 11.5 cm. Has a white stripe on its neck.

Sand Martin. 12 cm. Has brown back and collar. Nests in holes in banks.

House Martin. 12.5 cm. Has a white rump and a shorter tail than the Swallow. Often nests in large groups.

Swallow. 19 cm. Has long tail feathers and a dark throat. Feeds on insects.

Swift. 16.5 cm. Has very long curved wings.

Blackbird-sized Birds

The birds inside this panel are all drawn to the same scale.

Adult

Male

Juvenile

Female

Starling. 21.5 cm. On the ground has an upright way of walking. Often seen in large flocks.

Blackbird. 25 cm. The male is all black with an orange beak. The female is brown with a brown beak.

Song Thrush. 23 cm. Both sexes look the same, with a brown back and spotted breast. Often feeds on snails.

Mistle Thrush. 27 cm. A greyer bird than the Song Thrush and the spots on the breast are larger and closer together.

Remember—if you cannot see a picture of the bird you want to identify on these pages, turn to the page earlier in the book which deals with the kind of place where you saw the bird.

Adult   Juvenile

Robin. 14 cm. Can be very tame. Has an orange breast.

Female
Male
Bullfinch. 14.5–16 cm. Has a black cap, white rump and short black bill.

Female
Male
Greenfinch. 14.5 cm. Has yellow wing bars and a greenish rump.

Goldfinch. 12 cm. Has a red face and a black and white head.

Dunnock. 14.5 cm. Feeds on the ground and moves slowly with a kind of creeping walk.

Male   Female
House Sparrow. 14.5 cm. A very common bird. The male has a grey and brown head and black throat.

Tree Sparrow. 14 cm. Has a brown head and a black spot on its white cheeks. Likes to nest in old trees.

Male   Female
Chaffinch. 15 cm. Has white wing bars and white outer tail feathers.

Pied Wagtail   White Wagtail
Kingfisher. 16.5 cm. Catches small fish for food.

The **Pied Wagtail** (18 cm.) lives in Britain, the **White** (18 cm.) in Europe.

Skylark. 18 cm. Has white outer tail feathers.

Male   Female
Yellowhammer. 16.5 cm. The male has a yellow head.

Male   Female
Linnet. 13.5 cm. The male has a red forehead and chest.

Adult   Juvenile
Great Spotted Woodpecker. 23 cm. Has large white wing patches and a black line from beak to neck.

Juvenile   Adult
Green Woodpecker. 32 cm. Has a bright red head and yellow rump. Often feeds on ants on the ground.

Cuckoo. 33 cm. Has a long tail. It lays its eggs in the nests of other birds.

Male   Female
Kestrel. 34 cm. The commonest falcon. Often seen hovering over fields before dropping onto its prey.

Remember—if you cannot see a picture of the bird you want to identify on these pages, turn to the page earlier in the book which deals with the kind of place where you saw the bird.

Crow-sized Birds

The birds inside this panel are all drawn to the same scale.

Collared Dove. 32 cm. Has a black half collar at the back of the neck.

Woodpigeon. 41 cm. Has a white patch on each side of the neck.

Buzzard. 51–56 cm. Has broad wings and tail. Plumage varies from pale to dark.

Barn Owl. 34 cm. A large white-looking owl. It hunts in twilight or at night. The remains of food can be found as pellets.

Lapwing. 30 cm. Has a thin crest and broad, black and white wings which show up when it is flying.

Breeding plumage (summer)

Herring Gull. 56–66 cm. Commonest gull on the coast. Has a large yellow beak with a red spot near the tip and grey wings.

Non-breeding plumage (winter)

Black-headed Gull. 35–38 cm. In winter, instead of a dark head, it has only a dark mark behind the eyes.

Mallard-sized Birds

The birds inside this panel are all drawn to the same scale.

Coot. 38 cm. Larger than a Moorhen. Is all black with a white beak and forehead. Likes large, open stretches of water.

Moorhen. 33 cm. Its beak is red and the underside of its tail white. Swims with a jerky movement.

Breeding plumage (summer)

Non-breeding plumage (winter)

Great Crested Grebe. 48 cm. The largest grebe. In summer, has brownish frills round the neck. In winter, blackish ear tufts.

←Female

Male

Tufted Duck. 43 cm. The most common diving duck. The male has a long drooping crest, the female is browner with a much smaller crest. Forms large flocks on lakes and reservoirs.

Female

Male

Mallard. 58 cm. The male has a green head, white collar and purple-brown breast. Both birds have a blue patch and white bars on their wings, which show up best in flight.

30

Hooded

Carrion

Jackdaw. 33 cm. Has a grey head and is smaller than the all-black crows.

Magpie. 46 cm. A large bird with a long tail and black and white plumage.

The northern form of the **Carrion Crow** has black and grey feathers. It is called the **Hooded Crow** (47 cm.)

Rook. 46 cm. Has a thinner beak than the crow, with a bare white face.

Male

Female

Curlew. 51–58 cm. Largest wader. Has a long downward curved beak, a brown body, and long legs.

Pheasant. Male 66–89 cm. Female 53–63 cm. A large game-bird. The male is brightly coloured, the female browner with a shorter tail.

Larger Birds

These birds are not drawn to the same scale.

Whooper Swan

Juvenile Mute Swan

Female Mute Swan

Male Mute Swan

Bewick's Swan

Grey Heron. 90 cm. A large grey bird often seen standing at the water's edge. The nest is usually built in a tree.

Cormorant. 90 cm. Has a white chin and cheeks. Often seen sitting on rocks with its wings half-open.

Mute Swan. 152 cm. Has an orange bill with a black knob at the base. Swims with its neck curved.

Bewick's and Whooper Swan. 122 and 152 cm. Bewick's has a shorter bill with a smaller yellow patch. Both hold their necks stiffly when swimming.

Birds in Flight

Here are some illustrations to help you identify birds in flight. The sizes given are beak-to-tail measurements.

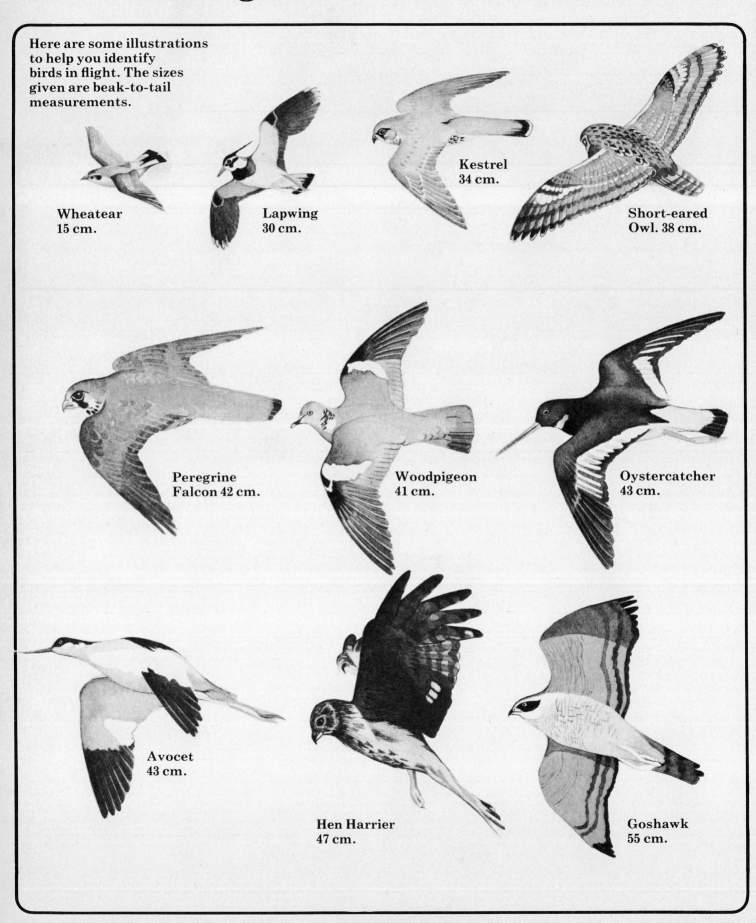

Wheatear
15 cm.

Lapwing
30 cm.

Kestrel
34 cm.

Short-eared
Owl. 38 cm.

Peregrine
Falcon 42 cm.

Woodpigeon
41 cm.

Oystercatcher
43 cm.

Avocet
43 cm.

Hen Harrier
47 cm.

Goshawk
55 cm.

Buzzard
54 cm.

Osprey
54 cm.

Black Kite
56 cm.

Herring Gull
60 cm.

Mallard
58 cm.

White-tailed
Eagle 69–91 cm.

Greylag Goose
76–89 cm.

White Stork
102 cm.

Pheasant
66–89 cm.

Mute Swan
152 cm.

Silver Birch

Part 2 written by Ingrid Selberg

Consultant Editor E. H. M. Harris, Director of the Royal Forestry Society

Norway Maple

Red Horse Chestnut

Apples

Part 2 TREES

Trees are around you everywhere: in gardens and parks, along city streets and in the countryside. Trees are one of the easiest living things to see.

This section is about common trees and how to study them. It shows you the different parts of a tree—the leaves, buds, flowers, fruits, bark and wood—and it explains how they work. It also shows you how each of these parts can help you to identify the tree. It tells the whole life story of a tree, from when it sprouts from a seed to when it dies from disease or is cut down for timber.

The best way to learn about how a tree grows is by growing one yourself. Page 50 shows you how to do this in easy-to-follow, step-by-step pictures.

If you want to identify a tree, look first at the illustrations on pages 60–65, or look on the pages which deal with the part of the tree that you are looking at. Remember that there are many clues to help you to identify a tree, not just its leaves, so try to use more than one.

Once you can recognize some common trees, try to find some rarer ones. A good place to look is in parks and in botanical gardens.

Making a tree survey, as described on pages 58–59, is great fun to do with a friend and it is a good way to test your skills as a tree detective.

If you take specimens from a tree, to put in a collection or to study at home, make sure you ask the permission of the owner.

Always use pruning shears to cut off twigs, never break them off. And, if you must climb trees, be very careful not to damage the trees or to hurt yourself.

Sitka Spruce

How to Identify Trees

When you want to identify a tree, the first things to look at are its leaves. But there are some trees whose leaves are very similar – for example, a Lombardy Poplar leaf could be confused with a Birch leaf. So always use at least one other feature, such as the flowers or bark, to help you identify a tree. (See pictures below.)

Trees can be divided into three groups: broadleaved, coniferous, and palm trees (see right). Try to decide to which group your tree belongs.

There is something to help you identify trees in every season. In spring and summer, look at the leaves and flowers. In autumn, many trees bear fruits which are good clues for identification. Winter is the best time to study buds, twigs, bark and tree shapes.

You do not need to go into a forest to find trees. Look at the many different kinds that grow in gardens, roads and in parks. Sometimes you can find rare trees in gardens.

Broadleaved Trees

Oak (summer)

Beech (spring)

Lime (winter)

Beech leaf and flower

Japanese Maple (autumn)

Most broadleaved trees have wide, flat leaves which they drop in winter. Some broadleaved trees, however, such as Holly, Laurel, Holm Oak and Box, are evergreen and keep their leaves in winter.

Broadleaved trees have seeds that are enclosed in fruits. The timber of broadleaved trees is called hardwood, because it is usually harder than the wood of most conifers, or softwood trees.

Tree or Shrub?

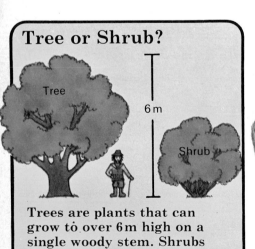

Tree

6 m

Shrub

Trees are plants that can grow to over 6m high on a single woody stem. Shrubs are generally smaller, and have several stems. See page 59 for how to measure trees.

What to Look for

Leaves

Yew (Conifer)

Oak (Broadleaf)

Beech (Broadleaf)

The leaves will give you the biggest clue to the identity of the tree, but look at other parts of the tree as well. There is a guide to leaves on page 40.

Shape and Bark

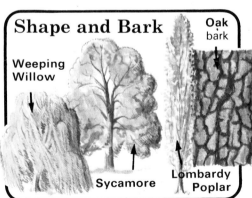

Oak bark

Weeping Willow

Sycamore

Lombardy Poplar

The overall shape of the tree, and of its top, or crown, are also good clues. Some trees can be recognized just by looking at their bark. See pages 44-5.

Conifers

Norway Spruce

Palms

Leaf

Scots Pine

Cone and needles

European Larch (in winter)

European Larch (in summer)

Canary Palm

Most conifers have narrow, needle-like or scaly leaves, and are evergreen. The Larch is one conifer that is not evergreen. Conifer fruits are usually woody cones, but some conifers, like the Yew, have berry-like fruits. The overall shape of conifers is more regular than that of most broadleaved trees.

Palms have trunks without branches that look like giant stalks. The leaves grow at the top of the tree. Unlike other trees, the Palm grows taller, without getting thicker.

Winter Buds

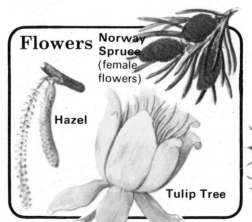

Beech

Sycamore

Oak

In winter, when there are no leaves to look at, you can still identify some trees from their buds, bark and shape. See page 43 for a guide to bud shapes.

Flowers

Norway Spruce (female flowers)

Hazel

Tulip Tree

In certain seasons trees have flowers which can help you to recognize the tree. But some trees do not flower every year. See pages 46-7.

Fruits and Seeds

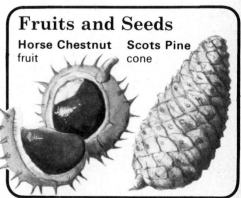

Horse Chestnut fruit

Scots Pine cone

All trees have fruits bearing seeds which may grow into new trees. This Horse Chestnut 'conker' and pine cone are both fruits. See pages 48-9.

How a Tree Grows

This is the life story of a Sycamore, but all trees grow in a similar way. Although there are many different kinds of trees, they all sprout from seeds, grow larger, flower, form fruits and shed seeds.

There are many stages of a tree's life story that you can study. You can watch it sprout from a seed and then chart its growth. You can count the girdle scars on a young tree to find out how old it is.

Older trees all have flowers and fruits at some time in most years, although they may be hard to see on some trees. They are not all as large as the Horse Chestnut's flowers or the fruit of the Apple tree. Not all fruits ripen in autumn. Some appear in early summer and even in spring.

An important part of a tree that you do not see is the roots. If you find an overturned tree, look at the roots and try to measure them. Look also at logs and tree stumps for the layers of wood and bark. They can tell you the age of the tree and its rate of growth.

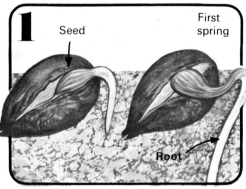

The tree starts growing in spring from a seed which has been lying in the soil all winter. Now, with the help of the food stored inside it, the seed sends down a root into the soil to suck up water and minerals.

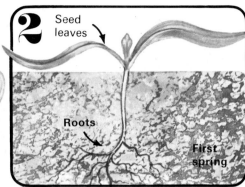

Then the seed sends up a shoot which pokes above the ground and into the light. Two fleshy seed leaves open up with a small bud between them. These leaves are not the same shape as the tree's ordinary leaves will be.

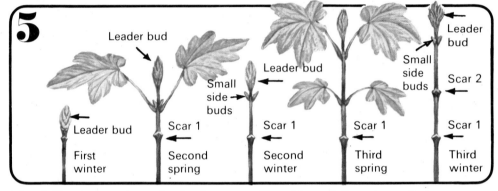

The following spring, the bud opens and a new shoot grows, with leaves at the tip. In autumn, they drop off. The next year, the same thing happens, and each year when the leaves fall off, they leave a girdle scar on the stem. Buds on the sides of the stem also grow shoots in the summer. But they do not grow as fast as the leader shoot at the top of the tree. Each year the tree grows taller, and the roots grow deeper.

When the tree is about twelve years old, it grows flowers on its branches in the spring. Bees, searching for nectar, visit the flowers and some of the pollen from the flowers sticks on to their hairy bodies.

When the bees visit other Sycamore flowers, some of the pollen on their bodies rubs off on to the female parts of the flowers. When the male (pollen) and female parts are joined, the flowers are fertilized and become fruits.

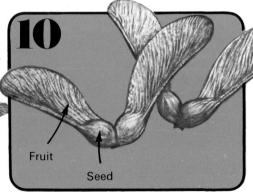

Later that year, the fruits fall off the tree, spinning like tiny helicopters, carrying the seeds away from the parent tree. The wings rot on the ground, and the seeds are ready to grow the following spring.

3

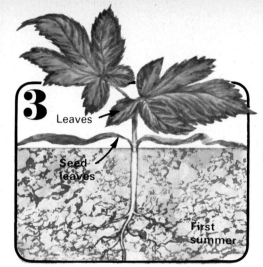

Leaves

Seed leaves

First summer

The seed leaves have stored food in them to help the tree grow. Soon the bud opens, and the first pair of ordinary leaves appears. The seed leaves then drop off. The roots grow longer.

4

Bud

First autumn and winter

Girdle scar

Bud

In the autumn, all the leaves change colour and drop off, leaving a "girdle scar" around the stem where they were attached, and a bud at the end of the shoot. The bud does not grow during the winter.

Holly leaf

Many broadleaved trees are deciduous, which means that they lose their leaves in autumn. They do this because their leaves cannot work properly in cold weather, and there is not enough sunlight in winter for the leaves to make food for the tree.

Most conifers are called evergreens because they keep their leaves throughout the winter. Their needles are tougher than most broadleaves, and they can keep making food even in the dark of winter.

A few broadleaved trees, such as Holly, are also evergreen. Like conifer needles, their leaves have a waxy coating which helps them survive the winter.

6

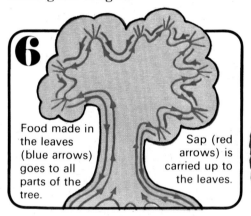

Food made in the leaves (blue arrows) goes to all parts of the tree.

Sap (red arrows) is carried up to the leaves.

The tree makes food for itself in its leaves, which contain a green chemical called chlorophyll. In sunlight, the chlorophyll can change air, water and minerals brought up from the soil into food for the tree.

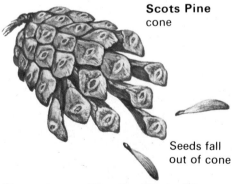

Scots Pine cone

Seeds fall out of cone

Some trees, like the Scots Pine, have fruits called cones, which stay on the tree, but open up to let the seeds fall out by themselves. When the cones are old and dried up, they usually fall off the tree too.

7

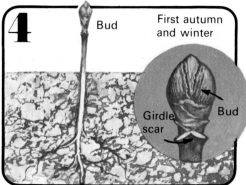

4

5

6

2

3

1

1

Bark is the outer layer which protects the tree from sun, rain and fungi which might attack it.

2

Tubes. Just inside the bark are tubes which carry food down from the leaves to all parts of the tree including the roots.

3

Cambium. This layer is so thin that you can hardly see it. Its job is to make a new layer of sapwood each year. This makes the trunk thicker and stronger.

4

Sapwood. This layer also has tiny tubes in it which carry the sap (water and minerals) to all parts of the tree from the roots. Each year a new "ring" of this wood is made by the cambium.

5

Heartwood. This is old sapwood which is dead and has become very hard. It makes the tree strong and rigid.

6

Rays. In a cross-section of a log you can see pale lines. These are called rays and they carry food sideways.

Each year the tree bears more branches. The stem thickens to hold them up, and the roots grow deeper and wider. The stem adds a new layer of wood. This picture shows you the inside of the stem, or trunk, and its different parts.

Leaves

The first thing that most people notice about a tree is its leaves. A big Oak tree has more than 250,000 leaves and a conifer may have many millions of needles.

The leaves fan out to the sunlight, and with the green chlorophyll inside them, they make food for the tree. They take in gases from the air and give out water vapour through tiny holes. Once the food is made, it is carried through veins to other parts of the leaf. The veins also strengthen the leaf like a skeleton.

The leaf stem brings water from the twig and also helps the leaf to move into the light. It is tough so that the leaf does not break off in strong winds.

Although the leaves of conifers and broadleaved trees look different, they both do the same work. Most conifer leaves can survive the winter, but broadleaves fall off in the autumn. Conifers also lose their leaves, but not all at once. A pine needle stays on a tree for about three to five years.

TRACKING DOWN YOUR MYSTERY LEAF

1. DECIDE IF THE LEAF IS FROM A CONIFER OR A BROADLEAVED TREE.
2. LOOK AT ITS SHAPE AND ITS EDGE.
3. NOTICE THE WAY THE LEAVES ARE ARRANGED ON THE TWIG.
4. LOOK AT THE COLOUR AND LEAF SURFACE.

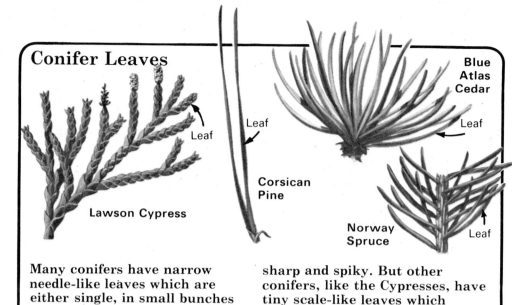

Conifer Leaves

Lawson Cypress — Leaf

Corsican Pine — Leaf

Blue Atlas Cedar — Leaf

Norway Spruce — Leaf

Many conifers have narrow needle-like leaves which are either single, in small bunches or in clusters. They can be very sharp and spiky. But other conifers, like the Cypresses, have tiny scale-like leaves which overlap one another.

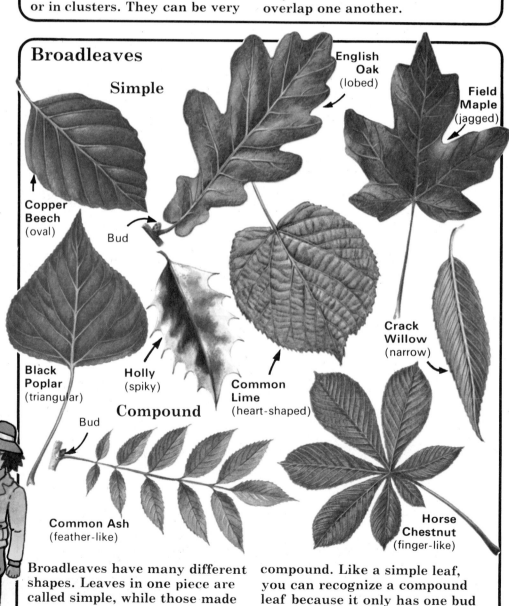

Broadleaves

Simple

Copper Beech (oval)

English Oak (lobed)

Field Maple (jagged)

Bud

Black Poplar (triangular)

Holly (spiky)

Common Lime (heart-shaped)

Crack Willow (narrow)

Compound

Bud

Common Ash (feather-like)

Horse Chestnut (finger-like)

Broadleaves have many different shapes. Leaves in one piece are called simple, while those made up of many leaflets are called compound. Like a simple leaf, you can recognize a compound leaf because it only has one bud at the base of its stem.

These leaves are not drawn to the same scale.

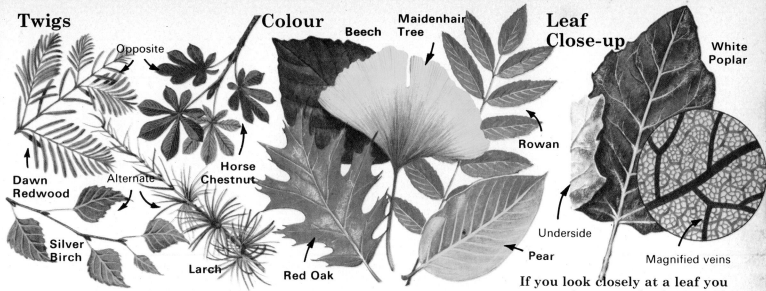

Twigs

Dawn Redwood, Opposite, Alternate, Horse Chestnut, Silver Birch, Larch

Leaves are arranged on twigs in various ways. They can be opposite each other in pairs, or they can be single and alternate from one side of the twig to the other.

Colour

Beech, Maidenhair Tree, Rowan, Red Oak, Pear

Leaves are green because of the chlorophyll inside them. In autumn, the chlorophyll in broadleaves decays. They change colour before they fall.

Leaf Close-up

White Poplar, Underside, Magnified veins

If you look closely at a leaf you can see its network of veins. The leaf's upper surface is tough and often glossy to stop the sun from drying out the leaf. The underside is often hairy.

Leaf Scrapbook

Leaf skeleton

Keep a notebook of the leaves you find. Place each leaf between two sheets of paper. Then put them between books with a heavy object on top. Leave them for a week. When the leaves are flat and dry, mount them in a notebook with tiny pieces of sellotape. Label the leaves and write down where and when you found them. You may also find leaf skeletons, from which the dried leaf has crumbled away, leaving only the strong stem and veins.

Leaf Tiles

Press the leaf on to the "clay" with a rolling pin.

The finished tile can be painted or varnished.

Make your clay by mixing together:
2 cups flour (not self-raising)
1 cup salt
1 cup water
2 tablespoons cooking oil
Shape your "clay" into a ball. Roll it out with a rolling pin until it is about 2 cm thick. Press your leaf, vein side down, on to the clay so that it leaves a mark. Remove the leaf and bake in the oven at Gas Mark $\frac{1}{2}$ (250°F) for about two hours.

Winter Buds

Most broadleaved trees have no leaves in winter, but you can still identify them by their winter buds.

A winter bud contains the beginnings of next year's shoot, leaves and flowers. The thick, overlapping bud scales protect the shoot from the cold and from attack by insects. In places where winter is the dry season, the bud scales keep the new shoot from drying out. If the undeveloped leaf does not have bud scales, it may be covered with furry hairs to protect it.

In spring, when it gets warmer, the new shoot swells and breaks open the hard protective scales. Each year's shoot comes from a bud and ends by forming a new bud at the end of the growing season.

There are many buds on a twig. The leading bud, which is usually at the tip, contains the shoot which will grow most. The shoot becomes a twig and eventually a branch. The other buds hold leaves and flowers. They are also reserves in case the leading bud is damaged.

Inside a bud there are tiny leaves and flowers, all folded up. If you cut a bud in half and look at it through a lens, you can see the different parts.

Outer scales of bud

Flower

Leaf

This is a three-year-old Horse Chestnut twig. You can tell its age by counting the girdle scars. It has large brown buds in opposite pairs. The bud scales are sticky.

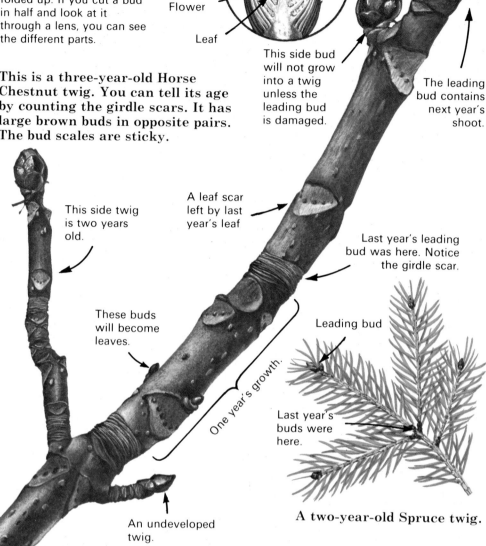

This side bud will not grow into a twig unless the leading bud is damaged.

The leading bud contains next year's shoot.

This side twig is two years old.

A leaf scar left by last year's leaf

Last year's leading bud was here. Notice the girdle scar.

These buds will become leaves.

One year's growth.

An undeveloped twig.

Leading bud

Last year's buds were here.

A two-year-old Spruce twig.

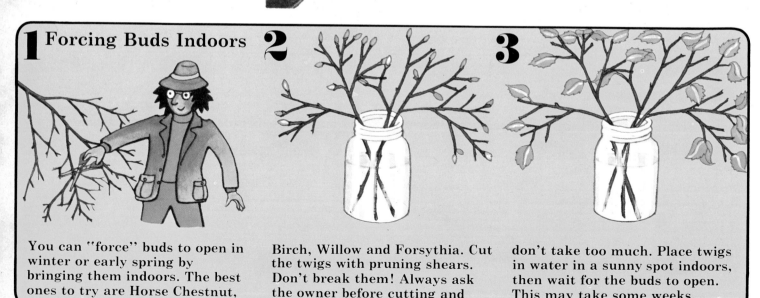

1 Forcing Buds Indoors

You can "force" buds to open in winter or early spring by bringing them indoors. The best ones to try are Horse Chestnut,

2

Birch, Willow and Forsythia. Cut the twigs with pruning shears. Don't break them! Always ask the owner before cutting and

3

don't take too much. Place twigs in water in a sunny spot indoors, then wait for the buds to open. This may take some weeks.

Winter Bud Identification Chart

What to Look for

If you try to identify trees by their winter buds, you will see that they vary a great deal. Here is a list of things to look for:

1 How are the buds positioned on the twig? Like leaves, buds can be in opposite pairs or single and alternate.
2 What colour are the buds and the twig?
3 What shape is the twig? Are the buds pointed or rounded?
4 Is the bud covered with hairs or scales? If there are scales, how many? Is the bud sticky?

Ash—Smooth, grey twig. Large, black buds opposite.

Sycamore— Large, green, opposite buds with dark-edged scales.

False Acacia—Grey twig. Thorns next to tiny, alternate buds.

Beech—Slender twig. Alternate, spiky, brown buds sticking out.

Elm—Zigzag twig. Alternate, blackish-red buds.

Willow—Slender twig. Alternate buds close to twig.

Lime—Zigzag twig. Alternate, reddish buds with two scales.

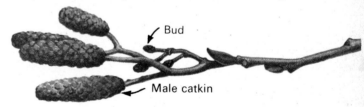

Bud

Male catkin

Alder—Alternate, stalked, purple buds often with male catkins.

Walnut—Thick, hollow twig. Big, black, velvety, alternate buds.

White Poplar—Twig and alternate buds covered with white down.

Turkey Oak—Clusters of alternate, whiskered buds.

Sweet Chestnut—Knobbly twig. Large, reddish, alternate buds.

Wild Cherry—Large, glossy, red buds grouped at tip of twig.

Plane—Alternate, cone-shaped buds. Ring scar around bud.

Magnolia—Huge, furry, green-grey buds.

Whitebeam—Downy, green, alternate buds.

These twigs are drawn life size.

Shape

Look at all these different tree shapes. Each type of tree has its own typical shape which depends on the arrangement of its branches. Winter is the best time of year to see the shapes of broadleaved trees because their branches are not hidden by leaves.

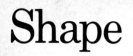

Practise making quick shape sketches when you are outside.

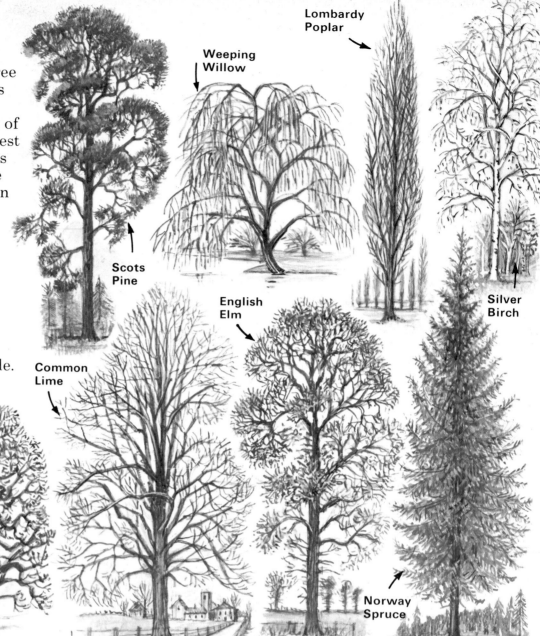

Weeping Willow

Lombardy Poplar

Scots Pine

English Elm

Silver Birch

Common Lime

Norway Spruce

English Oak

How Trees are Shaped

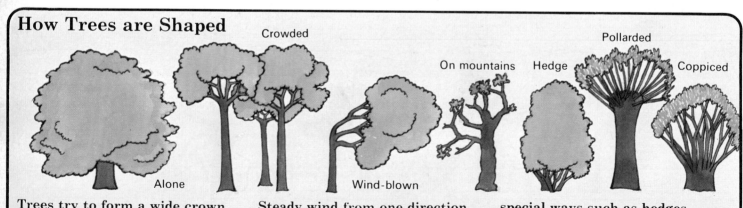

Crowded

Alone

Wind-blown

On mountains

Hedge

Pollarded

Coppiced

Trees try to form a wide crown or top so that their leaves will get lots of sunlight. Where trees are close together, they grow narrow to reach the light. Weather changes tree shapes.

Steady wind from one direction or salty sea winds make trees grow one-sided. On mountains, trees are dwarfed and gnarled by the cold and drying wind. Trees are also pruned or cut to grow in

special ways such as hedges. Pollarding means cutting off the branches of a tree. Coppicing is cutting the trunk down to the ground. This causes long, new shoots to grow.

Bark

The outside of the tree trunk is covered in a hard, tough layer of bark. It protects the inside of the tree from drying out and from damage by insects or animals. It also insulates the tree from extremes of heat and cold. Under the bark there are tubes carrying food (sap) which can be damaged if the bark is stripped off. If this happens, the tree may die.

When the tree is young the bark is thin and smooth, but with age it thickens and forms different patterns. You can identify trees by their bark.

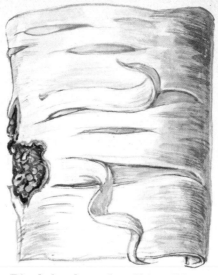

Birch bark peels off in ribbon-like strips.

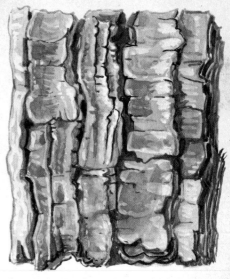

English Oak bark has deep ridges and cracks.

How Bark Patterns Form

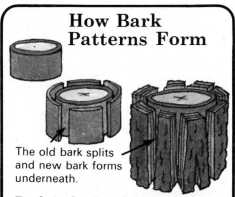

The old bark splits and new bark forms underneath.

Bark is dead and cannot grow or stretch. As wood inside the bark grows outwards, the bark splits, peels or cracks in a way that is special to each type of tree.

Scots Pine bark flakes off in large pieces.

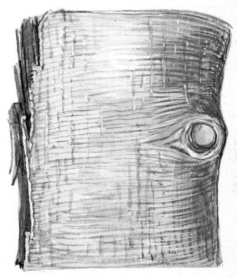

Beech has smooth thin bark, which flakes off in tiny pieces.

To make bark rubbings you need strong thin paper, sellotape and wax crayons or heel-ball. Tape the paper to the tree. Rub firmly with the crayon but do not tear the paper. Watch the bark pattern appear.

You can also rub the paper with candle wax. At home, paint over the rubbing. The bark pattern will stay white.

Cork

The bark on the Cork Oak is so thick that it can be removed without damaging the tree. Cork is used in many ways to keep in moisture and to resist heat.

Flowers

All trees produce flowers in order to make seeds that can grow into new trees. The flowers vary from tree to tree in size, shape and colour. Some are so small that you may not have noticed them.

Flowers have male parts called stamens and female parts called ovaries. The stamen produces pollen, while the ovary contains ovules. When pollen from the stamen reaches the ovules in the ovary, the flower is fertilized. Fertilized flowers grow into fruits (see pages 48-9), which contain seeds.

Flowers with both ovaries and stamens in the same flower, like the Cherry, are called perfect. On other trees the ovaries and the stamens are in separate flowers. Clusters of all-female flowers grow together and so do all-male flowers. The clusters can be cone-shaped or long and dangling (these are called catkins). A few trees, such as Yew, Holly and Willow, have their male and female flowers on entirely separate trees.

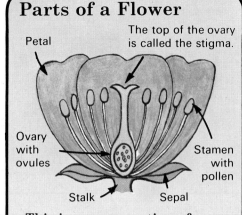

Parts of a Flower

Petal

The top of the ovary is called the stigma.

Ovary with ovules

Stamen with pollen

Stalk   Sepal

This is a cross-section of a Cherry blossom, which is a typical perfect flower. It has male and female parts.

European Larch

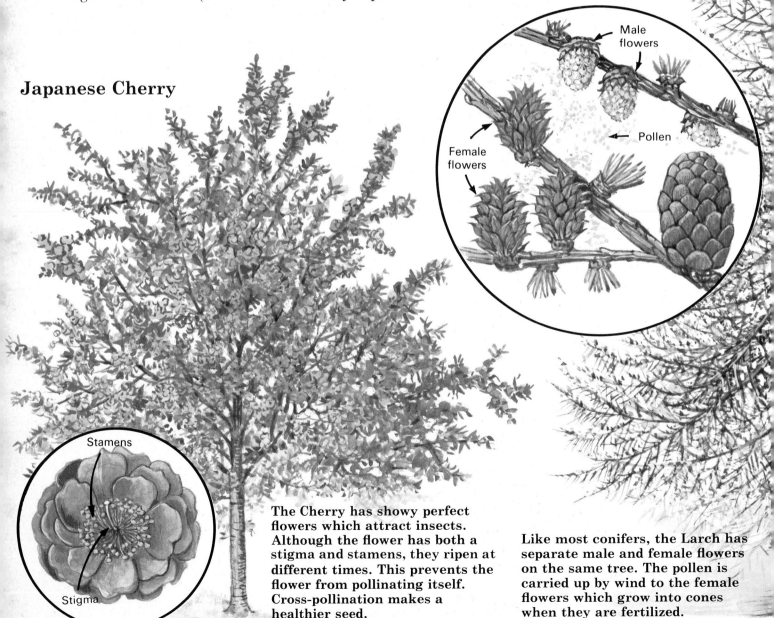

Male flowers

Pollen

Female flowers

Japanese Cherry

Stamens

Stigma

The Cherry has showy perfect flowers which attract insects. Although the flower has both a stigma and stamens, they ripen at different times. This prevents the flower from pollinating itself. Cross-pollination makes a healthier seed.

Like most conifers, the Larch has separate male and female flowers on the same tree. The pollen is carried up by wind to the female flowers which grow into cones when they are fertilized.

46

Pollination

Crab Apple

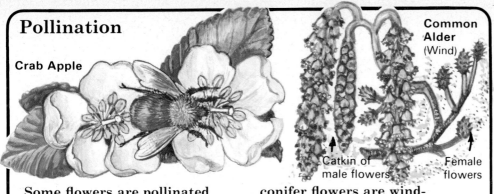

Common Alder (Wind)

Catkin of male flowers

Female flowers

Some flowers are pollinated by insects. Insects, feeding on flowers, accidentally pick up pollen on their bodies, and it rubs off on the next flower they visit. This is called cross-pollination. Most catkins and conifer flowers are wind-pollinated. They are small and dull because they do not need to attract insects. The wind blows pollen off the long stamens and the sticky stigmas catch the pollen.

Fertilization

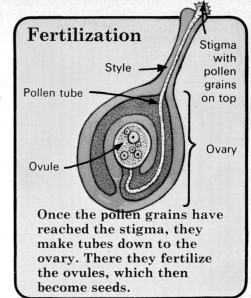

Stigma with pollen grains on top

Style

Pollen tube

Ovule

Ovary

Once the pollen grains have reached the stigma, they make tubes down to the ovary. There they fertilize the ovules, which then become seeds.

Crack Willow

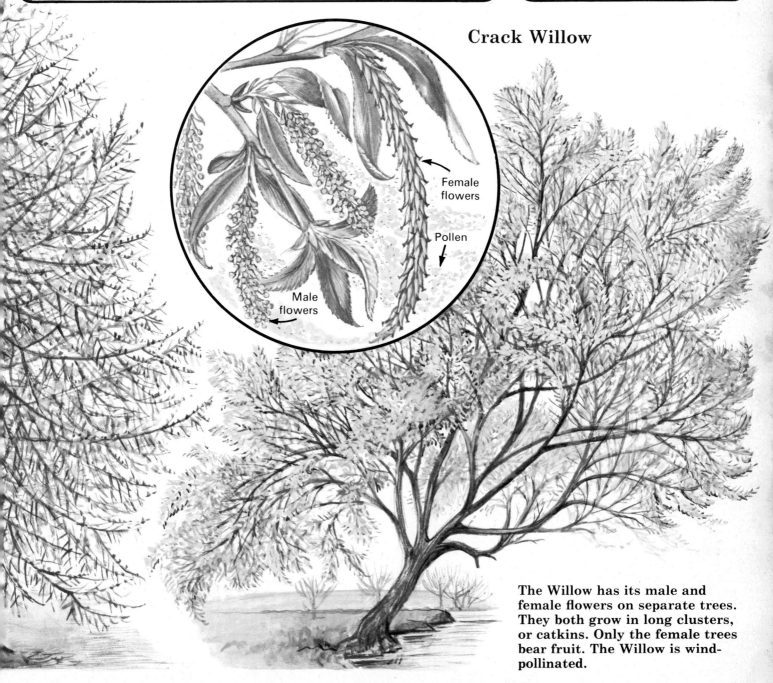

Female flowers

Pollen

Male flowers

The Willow has its male and female flowers on separate trees. They both grow in long clusters, or catkins. Only the female trees bear fruit. The Willow is wind-pollinated.

Fruits and Seeds

Fruits containing seeds grow from fertilized flowers. An Apple and the prickly conker case of the Horse Chestnut are both fruits. Although they look different, they do the same job. They protect the seeds they carry and help them to spread to a place where they can grow.

Conifers bear fruits whose seeds are uncovered, but which are usually held in a scaly cone. Broadleaved trees have fruits which completely surround their seeds. They take the form of nuts, berries, soft fruits, and many other kinds.

Many fruits and cones are damaged by insects and disease, are eaten by birds and animals, or fall off the trees before they can ripen. The seeds inside the remaining fruits ripen in the autumn. They need to get far away from the parent tree, or it will take all the food and light.

Seeds are spread by birds, animals, wind and water. Very few seeds ever get to a place where they can reach full growth. About one in a million acorns becomes an Oak tree.

How a Cone Ripens

The fertilized ovules become seeds.

Each scale holds two seeds.

Scale

Cross-section of a cone.

Cones develop from the female flowers. After pollination, the scales harden and close. The stalk often bends, so the cone hangs down. The cone turns from green to brown. When the seeds are ripe and the weather is warm and dry, the scales open. The seeds flutter out on papery wings. Most cones stay on the tree for a year. Others take two years to ripen, and some remain long after the seeds have been dropped.

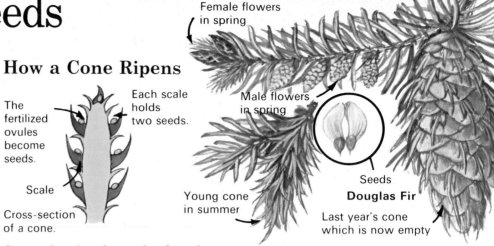

Female flowers in spring

Male flowers in spring

Young cone in summer

Seeds
Douglas Fir

Last year's cone which is now empty

Fruits of Conifers

Most cones have woody scales and vary in size from 1 cm to 35 cm and can weigh as much as 2 kg. See how many different kinds of cones you can collect.

Larch cones may stay on a tree for many years.

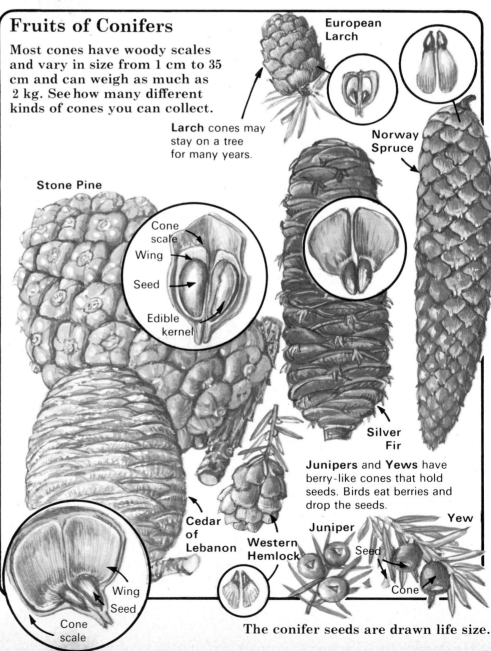

European Larch

Norway Spruce

Stone Pine

Cone scale
Wing
Seed
Edible kernel

Silver Fir

Junipers and **Yews** have berry-like cones that hold seeds. Birds eat berries and drop the seeds.

Cedar of Lebanon

Western Hemlock

Juniper

Yew

Seed

Cone

Wing
Seed
Cone scale

The conifer seeds are drawn life size.

Scots Pine

Cones open in warm, dry weather to release their seeds. If it is wet, the scales close. Find a cone and make it open by placing it near a heater. Then put it in a damp place, and it will close.

48

How a Peach Ripens

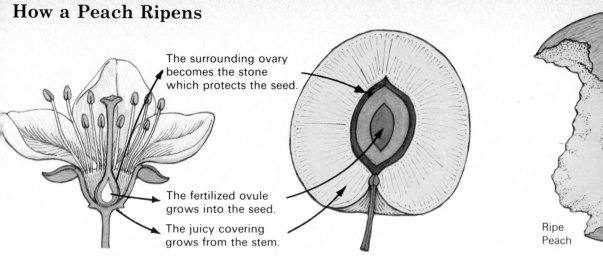

The surrounding ovary becomes the stone which protects the seed.

The fertilized ovule grows into the seed.

The juicy covering grows from the stem.

Ripe Peach

The pictures above show how the different parts of a flower grow into the different parts of a fruit. The flower is a Peach blossom.

Water from the stem and sunshine make the fleshy part of the fruit swell. As the fruit ripens, it turns golden pink and softens. The

bright colour and sweet smell attract hungry animals or people who eat the juicy outer layer and throw away the stone.

Fruits of Broadleaved Trees

Broadleaved trees produce many different kinds of fruits. Some are nuts with hard outer shells, some are soft fruits, some are pods, and some have wings or hairs.

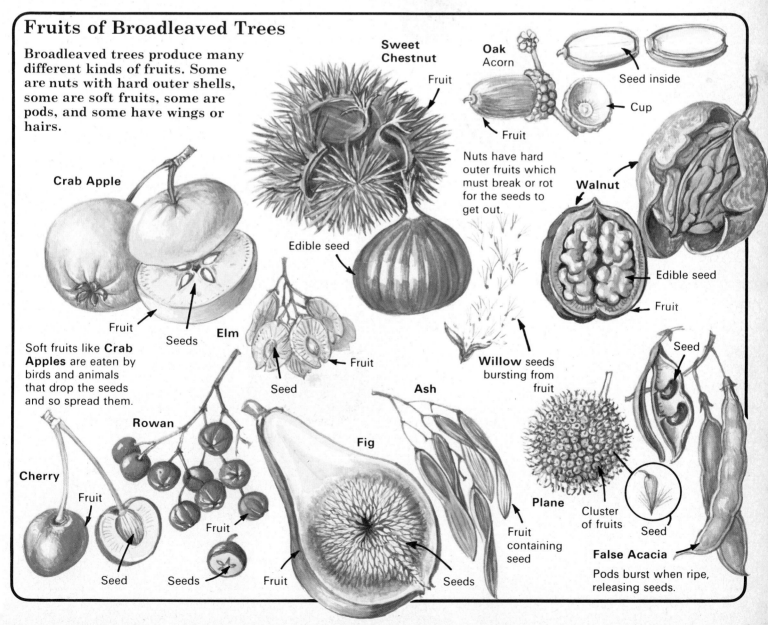

Sweet Chestnut
Fruit

Oak
Acorn
Fruit

Seed inside
Cup

Nuts have hard outer fruits which must break or rot for the seeds to get out.

Walnut
Edible seed
Fruit

Crab Apple
Fruit
Seeds

Edible seed

Soft fruits like **Crab Apples** are eaten by birds and animals that drop the seeds and so spread them.

Elm
Seed
Fruit

Willow seeds bursting from fruit

Seed

Cherry
Fruit
Seed

Rowan
Fruit
Seeds

Fig

Ash

Plane

Cluster of fruits

Seed

Fruit containing seed

Fruit
Seeds

Seed

False Acacia
Pods burst when ripe, releasing seeds.

The cones and fruits are drawn two thirds life size.

Grow Your Own Seedling

Try growing your own tree from a seed. Pick ripe seeds from trees or collect them from the ground if you know that they are fresh. The time a seed takes to sprout varies, but an acorn takes about two months. Some seeds, like those from conifers, may need to lie in the ground for over a year. Once your seedling has sprouted, keep a diary of its growth with drawings or photographs.

What You Need

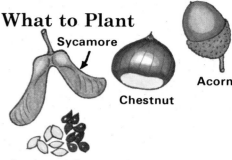

Flowerpots
Stones
String or rubber band
Plastic bags
Soil

What to Plant

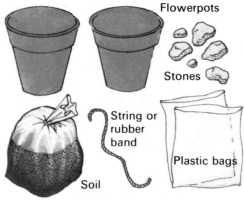

Sycamore
Chestnut
Acorn
Apple and Orange pips

Here are some seeds which are easy to grow. Acorns are usually successful, but try anything!

1

Soak acorns or other hard nuts in warm water overnight. Peel off the hard outer shells if you can, but do not try to cut the shells off acorns.

2

Put a handful of stones in the bottom of your pot. This is to help the water to drain properly. Place a saucer under the pot.

3

Put some soil, or compost, on top of the stones until the pot is about two thirds full. Water the soil until it is moist but not soggy.

4

Place the acorns or other seeds on top of the soil. They need lots of room to grow, so only put one acorn in each pot.

5

Cover the acorns or other seeds with a layer of soil about as thick as the seeds.

6

Fasten with string or rubber band.

Place a plastic bag over the pot and fasten it. This will keep the seed moist without watering. Put the pot in a sunny place and wait.

7

As soon as you see the seedling appear, remove the plastic bag. Water the seedling once or twice a week. The soil should be moist, but not wet.

8

Put your seedling outside in the summer if you can. In autumn, it will be ready to be planted in the ground (or you can leave it in its pot).

9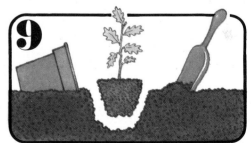

Dig a hole a bit larger than the pot. Gently scoop out the seedling and the soil around it from the pot. Plant it in the hole, pat down the soil on top, and water it.

Forestry

Trees have been growing on Earth for about 350 million years. The land was once covered by natural forests, but they have been cut down for timber and cleared for land. New forests are planted to replace the trees that are cut down.

Because conifers grow faster than broadleaved trees and produce straight timber, they are preferred for wood production.

Seedbeds

The seeds are sown in seedbeds. When the seedlings are 15-20 cm high, they are planted in rows in another bed where they have more room. They are weeded regularly.

Planting Out

When the seedlings are about 50 cm high, they are planted out in the forest ground, which has been cleared and ploughed. There are about 2,500 trees per hectare.

This picture and the two above show the story of a Douglas Fir plantation, and what the foresters do to care for the trees.

Fire towers on hills help to spot fire — the forest's worst enemy. Fires can be started by a carelessly dropped match or an unguarded campfire.

Trees can be sprayed with herbicides or treated with fertilizers from the air.

When the trees are felled, they are taken away to sawmills to be cut up.

Every few years the poorer trees are cut out to give more light and room to the stronger ones. These thinnings are used for poles or are made into paper pulp.

Dead and lower branches are cut off trees. This lessens the risk of fire and stops knots from forming in the wood.

Trees are felled when they are full-grown (about 70 years for conifers and 150 years for Oaks). About one in every ten trees reaches its full growth.

Annual Rings

Inside the bark is the wood which is made up of many layers (see page 39). Each year the cambium makes a ring of wood on its inner side and grows outwards. This layer is called an annual ring. The early wood made in spring is pale and has wide tubes to carry sap. Late wood, which is formed in summer, is darker and stronger. In wet years, the layers of wood are broad and the annual rings are far apart, but in dry years they are narrow. They are also narrow if the trees are not thinned.

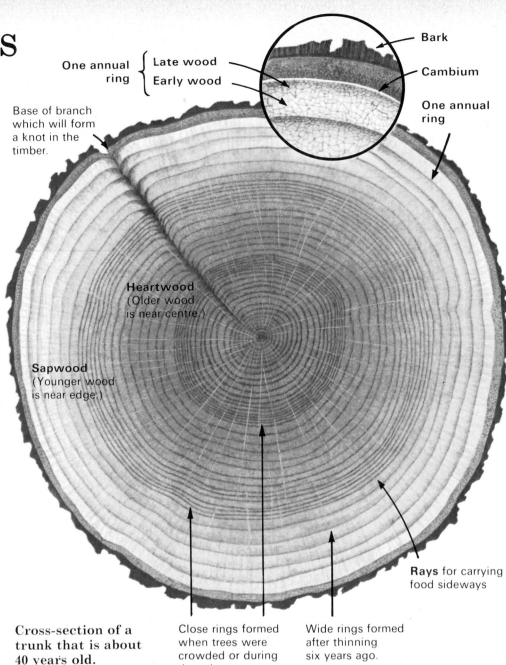

One annual ring { Late wood / Early wood

Bark

Cambium

One annual ring

Base of branch which will form a knot in the timber.

Heartwood (Older wood is near centre.)

Sapwood (Younger wood is near edge.)

Rays for carrying food sideways

Cross-section of a trunk that is about 40 years old.

Close rings formed when trees were crowded or during drought.

Wide rings formed after thinning six years ago.

Palms

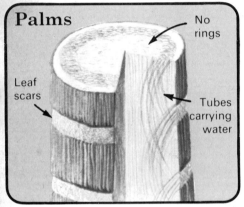

No rings

Leaf scars

Tubes carrying water

Palm trees do not have annual rings because they have no cambium to grow new wood. Their trunks are like giant stalks which do not grow thicker.

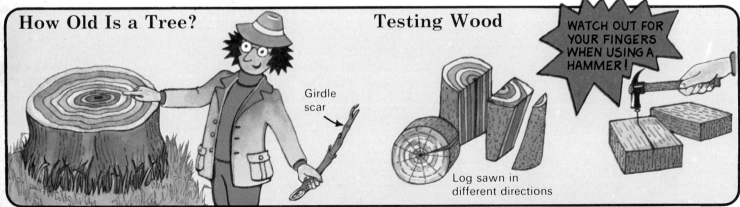

How Old Is a Tree?

Girdle scar

Testing Wood

WATCH OUT FOR YOUR FINGERS WHEN USING A HAMMER!

Log sawn in different directions

You can find out the age of a tree by counting the annual rings in a cross-section of its trunk. It is easiest to count the dark rings of late wood. Twigs also have annual layers. Cut off a twig on the slant and count its rings. Then count the girdle scars on the outside. Do they agree?

Saw a small log in different ways and look at the patterns the wood makes. Test the strength of different woods by hammering nails into them.

Wood

The wood inside different types of trees varies in colour and pattern just as their outside appearances vary. Different kinds of wood are especially suited for certain uses. Wood from conifers, called softwood, is mainly used for building and paper pulp, while broadleaved trees, called hardwoods, are used to make furniture.

At the sawmill, the person operating the saw decides the best way to cut each log. A log can be made into many different sizes of planks as well as into paper pulp.

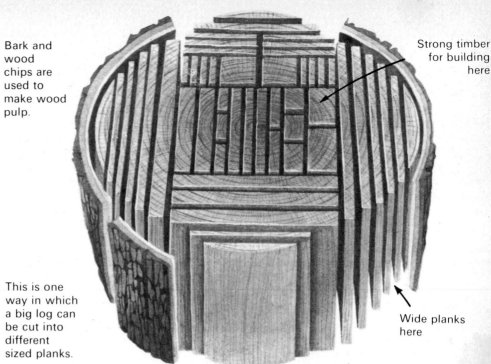

Bark and wood chips are used to make wood pulp.

Strong timber for building here

This is one way in which a big log can be cut into different sized planks.

Wide planks here

Grain

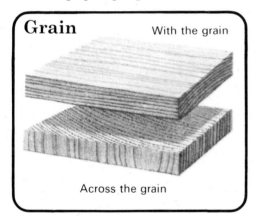

With the grain

Across the grain

When a plank is cut from a log, the annual rings make vertical lines which may be wavy or straight. This pattern is called the grain. Wood cut with the grain is stronger.

Knots

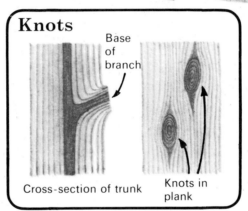

Base of branch

Cross-section of trunk

Knots in plank

In a plank you may see dark spots called knots. These were where the base of a branch was buried in the trunk of the tree. This distorts the grain, leaving a knot.

Seasoning

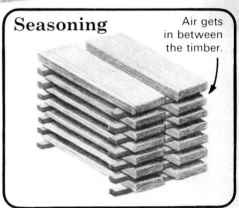

Air gets in between the timber.

Fresh wood contains water which is why green logs spit in the fire. As wood dries, it shrinks and often cracks or warps. Planks must be dried out, or seasoned, before they can be used.

Processed Wood

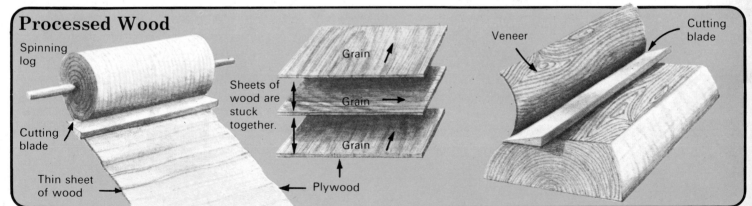

Spinning log

Cutting blade

Thin sheet of wood

Sheets of wood are stuck together.

Grain

Grain

Grain

Plywood

Veneer

Cutting blade

Much of the wood that you see around you has been 'processed'. Plywood is thin layers of wood which are glued together with the grain lying in different directions.

It is stronger than ordinary wood and does not warp. The thin sheet of wood is peeled off the log like a Swiss roll. Veneer is a thin sheet of wood with a beautiful grain

which is used on the surface of plain furniture. Chipboard (not shown) is made of small chips and shavings mixed with glue.

Pests and Fungi

Trees are attacked by insects and fungus diseases. Insects use trees for food, shelter and as places to breed. They can cause serious damage to trees, but they rarely kill them.

Fungi are a group of non-flowering plants which include mushrooms. Because fungi cannot make their own food, they may feed off other living things and sometimes kill them. Fungi spread by releasing microscopic seeds, called spores, into the air. If these spores get into the tree and spread, they will rot it.

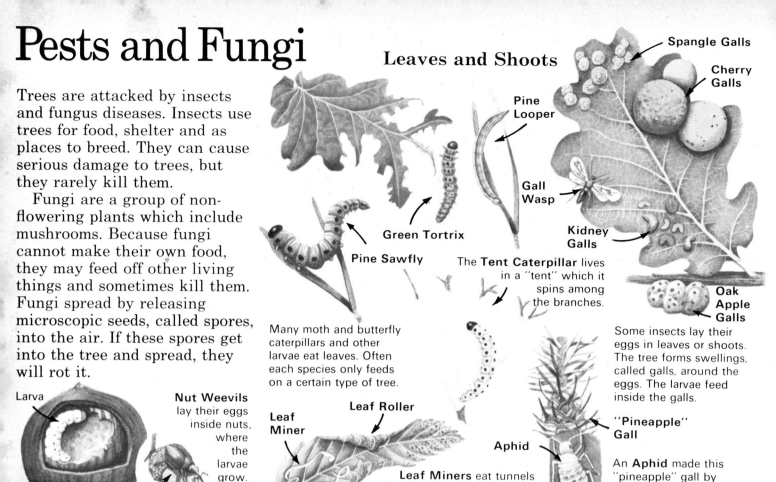

Leaves and Shoots

Spangle Galls

Cherry Galls

Pine Looper

Gall Wasp

Kidney Galls

Green Tortrix

Pine Sawfly

The **Tent Caterpillar** lives in a "tent" which it spins among the branches.

Oak Apple Galls

Some insects lay their eggs in leaves or shoots. The tree forms swellings, called galls, around the eggs. The larvae feed inside the galls.

Larva

Nut Weevils lay their eggs inside nuts, where the larvae grow.

Adult **Nut Weevil**

Many moth and butterfly caterpillars and other larvae eat leaves. Often each species only feeds on a certain type of tree.

Leaf Miner

Leaf Roller

Aphid

"Pineapple" Gall

An **Aphid** made this "pineapple" gall by piercing a shoot to suck out the sap.

Leaf Miners eat tunnels through leaves. **Leaf Rollers** fold leaves over themselves for protection.

Bark and Wood

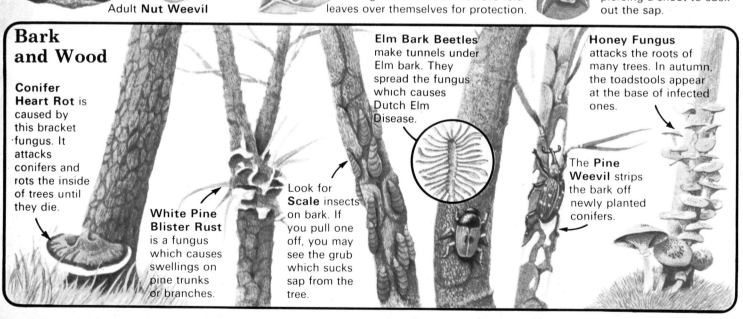

Conifer Heart Rot is caused by this bracket fungus. It attacks conifers and rots the inside of trees until they die.

White Pine Blister Rust is a fungus which causes swellings on pine trunks or branches.

Look for **Scale** insects on bark. If you pull one off, you may see the grub which sucks sap from the tree.

Elm Bark Beetles make tunnels under Elm bark. They spread the fungus which causes Dutch Elm Disease.

Honey Fungus attacks the roots of many trees. In autumn, the toadstools appear at the base of infected ones.

The **Pine Weevil** strips the bark off newly planted conifers.

Roots

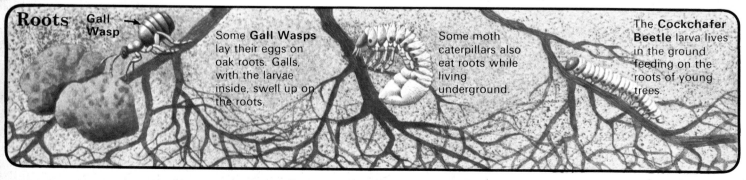

Gall Wasp

Some **Gall Wasps** lay their eggs on oak roots. Galls, with the larvae inside, swell up on the roots.

Some moth caterpillars also eat roots while living underground.

The **Cockchafer Beetle** larva lives in the ground feeding on the roots of young trees.

Keeping an Oak Gall

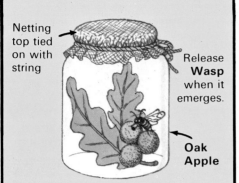

Netting top tied on with string

Release **Wasp** when it emerges.

Oak Apple

In summer, collect Oak Apples and other galls which do not have holes in them. Keep them in a jar with netting on top. The wasps living inside the galls should emerge in a month.

Making Spore Prints

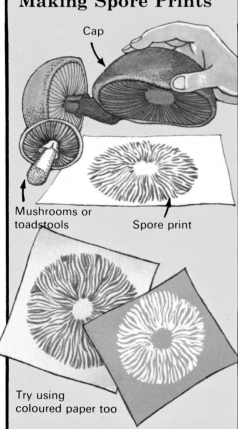

Cap

Mushrooms or toadstools

Spore print

Try using coloured paper too

Make spore prints from mushrooms. Cut off the stalk and place the cap on some paper. Leave it overnight. It will release its spores on the paper, leaving a print. Always wash your hands after handling fungus.

Bark stripped by a **Deer's** antlers

Tree struck by lightning

Bark gnawed by a **Field Vole**

Sometimes trees are damaged by animals. Deer strip the bark off trees when they scrape the "velvet" off their antlers. Squirrels, voles and rabbits eat young bark. If lightning strikes a tree, the trunk often cracks. This happens because the sap gets so hot that it becomes steam. It expands and then explodes, shattering the tree.

How a Tree Heals Itself

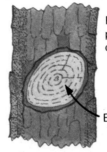

Recent pruning cut

Bare wood

Three years later

Six years later

New bark covering wound

If a branch is pruned off a tree properly, the wound usually heals. A new rim of bark grows from the cambium around the cut. This finished seal will keep out fungus and disease. It takes years for a wound to heal. But if a wound completely surrounds the trunk, the tree will die because its food supply is cut off.

How Trees Die

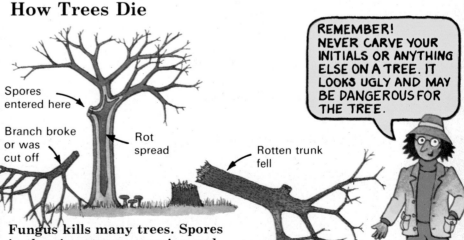

Spores entered here

Branch broke or was cut off

Rot spread

Rotten trunk fell

REMEMBER! NEVER CARVE YOUR INITIALS OR ANYTHING ELSE ON A TREE. IT LOOKS UGLY AND MAY BE DANGEROUS FOR THE TREE.

Fungus kills many trees. Spores in the air enter an opening and spread through the tree. The heartwood rots until the tree dies and falls down.

Woodland Life

When you walk in a forest, it may seem dead and deserted, but in its depths, the forest hides a wealth of life. Trees provide protection from bad weather, wind and too much sun. Tree roots help to hold the soil in place. Fallen leaves and twigs make a rich soil called humus. All this encourages plants to grow.

Trees also provide food and shelter for many animals. The plants and animals you find in coniferous and broadleaved forests are usually different, although they may overlap.

A Coniferous Forest

A coniferous forest is dark and dense. Few plants grow on the ground because of the thick layer of needles and the lack of light. Here are some animals and plants you might see in a coniferous forest.

Pine Marten

Squirrel's drey

Long-eared Owl's nest

Long-eared Owl

Great Spotted Woodpecker

Red Deer

Crossbill

Bracken

Fox

Black Grouse

Norway Spruce cones

Wood Ant-hill

Broad Buckler Fern

Timberman

Goldcrest

Fly Agaric

Red Squirrel

Lichen

Black Slug

Treecreeper

A Broadleaved Forest

A broadleaved forest is more light and open and so attracts many plants and animals. There are many flowers in spring before the trees' leaves have blocked out the light. As you can see, an Oak wood supports a great variety of life.

Mistletoe

Green Woodpecker

Nuthatch

Rook in nest

Tawny Owl

Long-eared Bat in tree

Poor Man's Beefsteak

Blue Tit

Oak

Roe Deer

Wood Anemone

Badger

Bluebells

Rabbit

Ivy

Pheasant

Hedgehog

Common Shrew

Primrose

Common Toad

Earthworm

Greater Stag Beetle

Speckled Wood Butterfly

Making a Tree Survey

Make a survey of the trees that grow around you. Choose a garden, street or park where you think there will be a variety of trees, but start with a small area first. It is easier and more fun to do this with a friend.

When you have decided on an area, make a rough map of it with any landmarks, such as roads or buildings. Try to work out a scale for your map. (It helps to use graph paper.) Work in a definite order so that you do not miss out any trees, and then go back to identify and measure them.

What to Take

Tape measure

Pencils

String

Notebook

Identifying a Tree

Try to identify the trees using this book or a field guide. Remember that there are many clues to help you recognize them, so don't use just one clue.

Making a Map

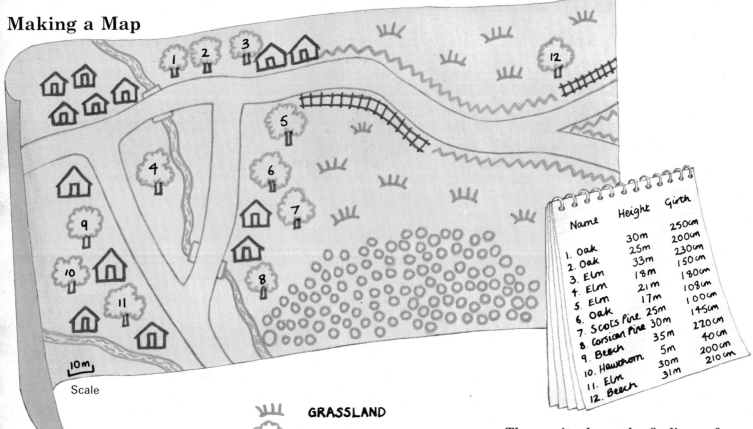

Scale 10m

Name	Height	Girth
1. Oak	30m	250cm
2. Oak	25m	200cm
3. Elm	33m	230cm
4. Elm	18m	150cm
5. Elm	21m	180cm
6. Oak	17m	108cm
7. Scots Pine	25m	100cm
8. Corsican Pine	30m	145cm
9. Beech	35m	220cm
10. Hawthorn	5m	40cm
11. Elm	30m	200cm
12. Beech	31m	210cm

After you have identified and measured the trees (as shown above), make a neater and more detailed copy of your map. Show the scale of your map. Then make a key to the symbols you used. Here are some suggestions:

GRASSLAND

TREE

WOODLAND

STREAM

BRIDGE

HOUSE

HEDGE

FENCE

Then write down the findings of your survey. Give the name, height and girth of each tree. Repeat the survey later to see if there are any new trees, or if anything has changed.

Measuring a Tree

Your friend is 1.5 m tall.

Mark stick here

The tree is four times the height of your friend. It is 6 m tall.

Ask your friend to stand next to the tree. Hold a stick up vertically at arm's length, and move your thumb up the stick until it is in line with your friend's feet, while the tip of the stick is in line with the top of your friend's head.

Mark the stick where your thumb is. See how many times the part of the stick above the mark goes into the height of the tree (four times here). Then multiply your friend's height (1.5 m here) by this number to get the height of the tree (6 m).

Measure around the tree at chest height to find the girth. Ask your friend to hold one end of some string while you hold the other. Walk around the tree until you meet. Then measure the length of string.

1 Studying a Tree

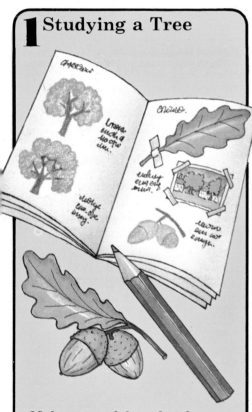

Make a careful study of one tree all through the year. Choose a tree which you can get to easily and often. Make a notebook in which you keep a record of when it comes into leaf, when it flowers and fruits, and when it drops its leaves. Include sketches or photos of the tree at these different times and specimens from it.

2

Study the animals that live in or near your tree. Look for birds' nests and squirrels' dreys in the tree top. Look on the trunk for insects and on the ground for other traces of animals, such as owl pellets, and nuts or cones which have been eaten by animals. To examine the insects in the tree top, beat a sturdy branch with a stick. Catch the insects that fall on a white sheet.

3

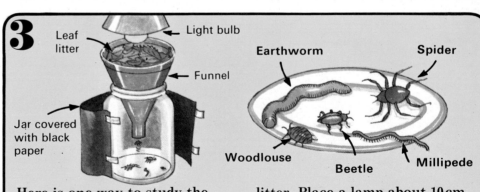

Leaf litter

Light bulb

Funnel

Jar covered with black paper

Earthworm

Spider

Woodlouse

Beetle

Millipede

Here is one way to study the animals which hide in the leaf litter on the ground. Take a large funnel (or make one out of tin foil), and place it in a jar. Cover the jar with black paper. Fill the funnel with damp leaf litter. Place a lamp about 10 cm above the leaves and switch it on. Wait a few hours. The heat and light from the lamp will drive the animals into the dark jar. You can take them out and study them.

Common Trees to Spot : Conifers

Lawson Cypress 25 m. Narrow shape. Drooping top shoot. Small, round cones. Common as hedge.

Western Red Cedar 30 m. Branches curve upwards. Tiny, flower-like cones. Hedges.

Yew 15 m. Dark green. Trunk gnarled. Bark reddish. Leaves and red-berried fruits poisonous.

Western Hemlock 35 m. Branches and top shoot droop. Small cones. Needles various lengths.

Norway Spruce 30 m. Christmas tree. Long, hanging cones. Parks, gardens, plantations.

Douglas Fir 40 m. Hanging, shaggy cones. Deep-ridged bark. Important timber tree.

European Silver Fir 40 m. Large, upright cones at top of tree. Parklands.

Scots Pine 35 m. Uneven crown. Bare trunk. Flaking bark. Common wild and planted.

Corsican Pine 36 m. Shape rounder and fuller than **Scots Pine**. Long, dark-green needles. Dark brown bark.

Blue Atlas Cedar 25 m. Broad shape. Barrel-shaped, upright cones. Blue-green needles. Parks.

European Larch 38 m. Upright cones egg-shaped. Soft, light-green needles fall off in winter.

Japanese Larch 35 m. Upright, rosette-like cones. Orange twigs. Blue-green needles fall off in winter.

Broadleaved Trees

The trees are arranged by leaf shape.
The height given is of a large, full-grown tree.

Olive 10 m. Evergreen. Twisted grey trunk. Black edible fruits. Southern Europe.

Holm Oak 20 m. Evergreen. Shiny leaves resemble Holly. Grey bark. Parks and gardens.

Weeping Willow 20 m. Drooping shape. Near water and in gardens.

Japanese Cherry 9 m. Flowers April–May. Many varieties. Gardens and along streets.

Wild Cherry or **Gean** 15 m. Red-brown bark peels in ribbons. Flowers April–May. Fruits sour. Woods, thickets.

Almond 8 m. Flowers March–April before leaves. Edible nut inside green fruit. Gardens.

Holly 10 m. Evergreen. Leaves often variegated. Berries poisonous. Often shrub-like.

Sweet Chestnut 35 m. Spiral-ridged bark. Two edible nuts in prickly green case. Wide-spreading branches.

Crab Apple 10 m. Small tree. Flowers May. Fruits edible but sour. Wild in hedges and thickets.

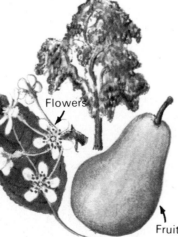

Common Pear 15 m. Straight trunk. Flowers April–May. Edible fruits. Hedgerows and gardens.

Orange 9 m. Evergreen. Many varieties. Fragrant flowers in winter. Fruits edible. Southern Europe.

Goat or **Pussy Willow** 7 m. Catkins March–April. Separate male and female trees. Hedges and damp woodlands.

Broadleaved Trees

Common Beech 25 m. Smooth, grey bark. Nuts eaten by animals. Leaves can also be purple-coloured.

Fruit / Flowers

Hornbeam 10 m. Smooth, grey, fluted trunk. Green winged fruits hanging in clusters. Hedges.

Male Flower

Wych Elm 20 m. Round, even crown. Woods and hedgerows. More common than **English Elm** in the north.

Fruits / Flowers / Fruits

English Elm 30 m. Tall narrow crown, often irregular shape. Hedgerows and woods. Attacked by Dutch Elm Disease.

Flowers / Fruits

Whitebeam 8 m. Leaves white-felted underneath. Flowers May–June. Sour red berries. Grows wild.

Flowers / Fruits

Black Poplar 25 m. Dark trunk often with bumps. Common in city parks.

Male Flower

Silver Birch 15 m. White bark peels in ribbons. 'Lamb's tail' catkins in April. Wild on heaths and mountains. Planted in gardens.

Female Flower / Male Flower

Common Alder 12 m. Cone-like fruits which stay on in winter. Catkins in early spring. Near water and damp woodlands.

Female Flowers / Male Flowers / Fruits

Common Lime 25 m. Heart-shaped leaves. Fragrant flowers attract bees in June. Parks and gardens.

Flowers / Fruits

Turkey Oak 25 m. Whiskers on buds and at base of leaves. Acorn cups mossy. Bark ridged.

Flowers / Fruit

English or **Pedunculate Oak** 23 m. Wide-spreading branches. Long-stalked acorns. Common alone and in woods.

Fruit / Flowers

White Poplar 20 m. Leaves covered with white down underneath. Bark whitish-grey with diamond marks.

Female Flower / Male Flower

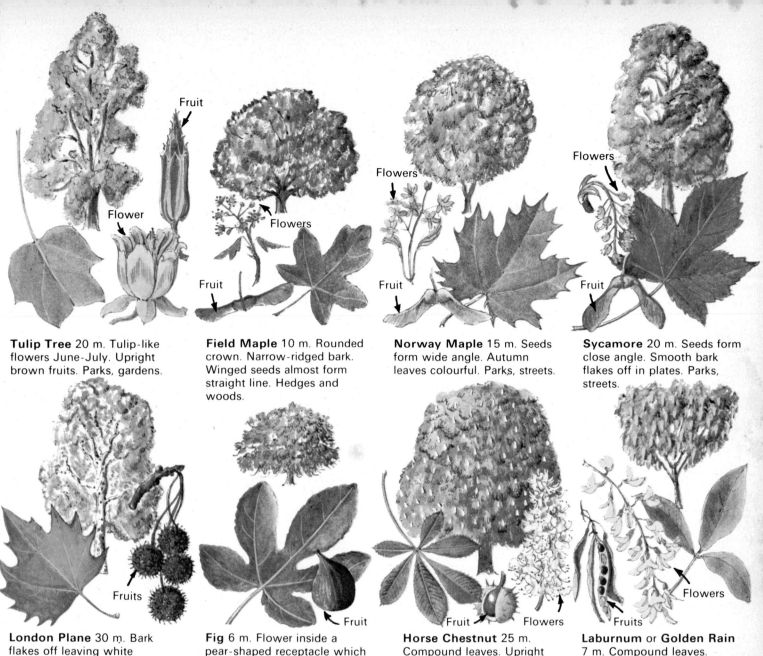

Tulip Tree 20 m. Tulip-like flowers June-July. Upright brown fruits. Parks, gardens.

Field Maple 10 m. Rounded crown. Narrow-ridged bark. Winged seeds almost form straight line. Hedges and woods.

Norway Maple 15 m. Seeds form wide angle. Autumn leaves colourful. Parks, streets.

Sycamore 20 m. Seeds form close angle. Smooth bark flakes off in plates. Parks, streets.

London Plane 30 m. Bark flakes off leaving white patches. Spiky fruits stay on in winter. City streets.

Fig 6 m. Flower inside a pear-shaped receptacle which becomes the fruit. Gardens.

Horse Chestnut 25 m. Compound leaves. Upright flowers May. Prickly fruits with 'conkers' inside.

Laburnum or **Golden Rain** 7 m. Compound leaves. Flowers May-June. Seeds poisonous. Gardens.

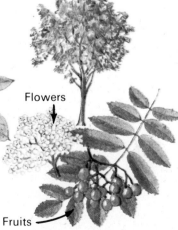

False Acacia or **Locust Tree** 20 m. Compound leaves. Ridged twigs spiny. Hanging flowers in June. Gardens, parks.

Walnut 15 m. Compound leaves. Deep-ridged bark. Hollow twigs. Edible nuts inside thick green fruits.

Rowan or **Mountain Ash** 7 m. Compound leaves. Flowers May. Sour orange berries September. Wild on mountains.

Common Ash 25 m. Compound leaves open late. Keys stay on in winter. Common in woods and parks.

Trees in Winter

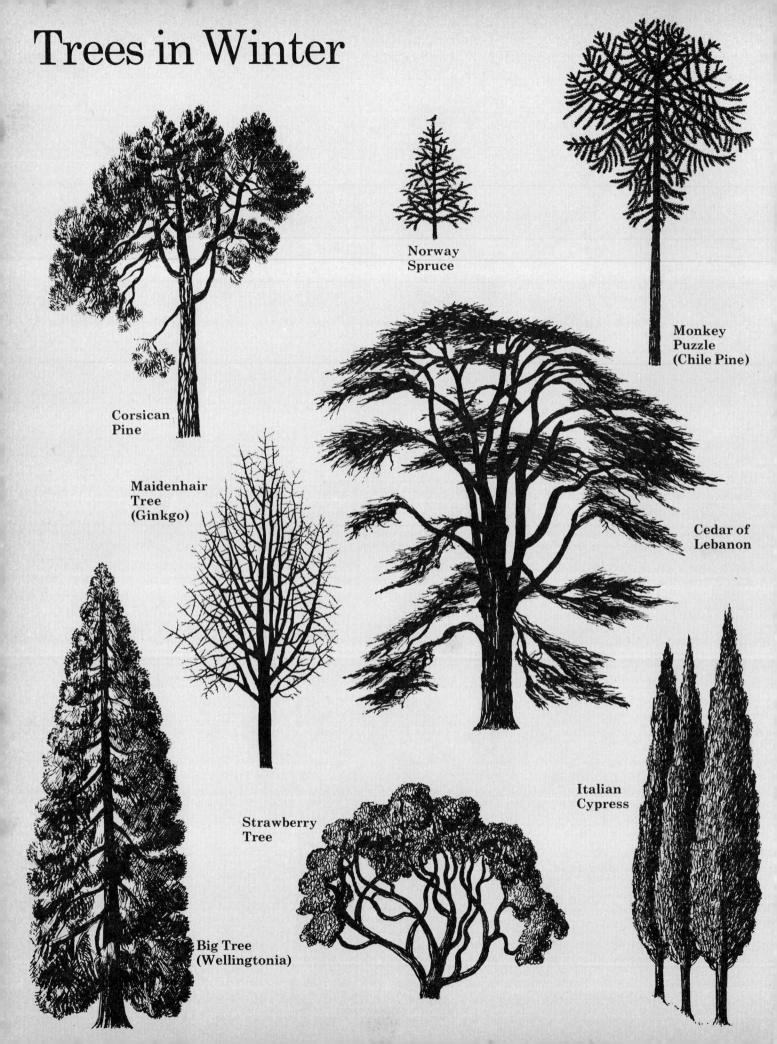

Norway Spruce

Monkey Puzzle (Chile Pine)

Corsican Pine

Maidenhair Tree (Ginkgo)

Cedar of Lebanon

Big Tree (Wellingtonia)

Strawberry Tree

Italian Cypress

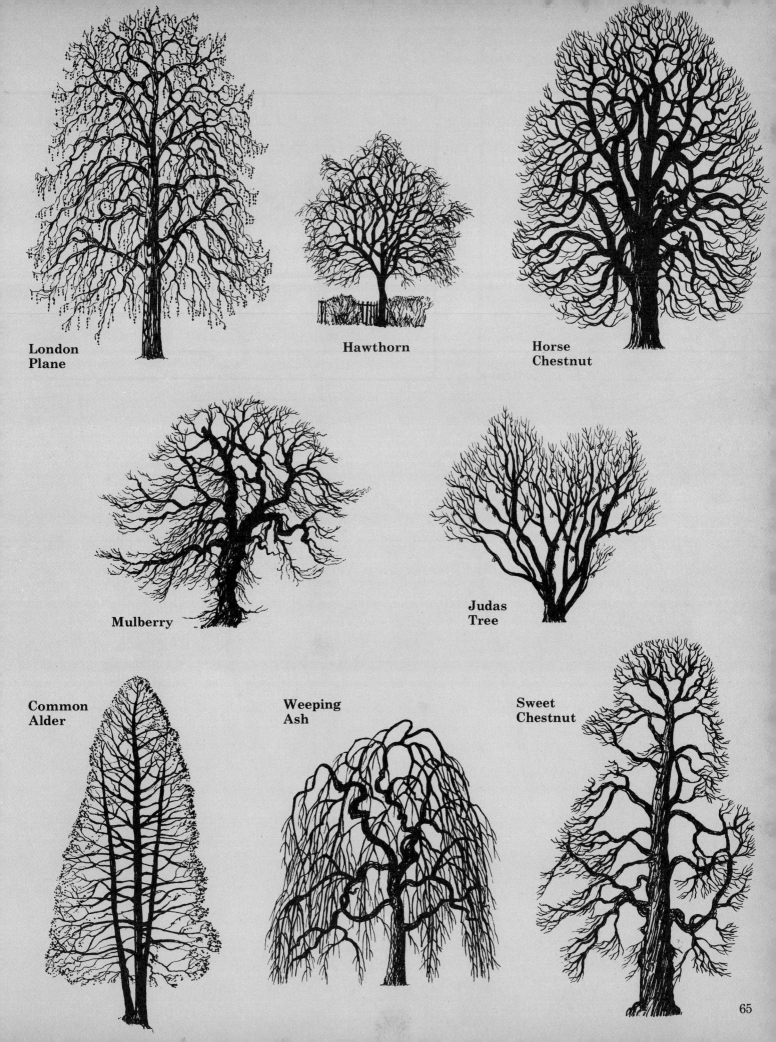

London
Plane

Hawthorn

Horse
Chestnut

Mulberry

Judas
Tree

Common
Alder

Weeping
Ash

Sweet
Chestnut

65

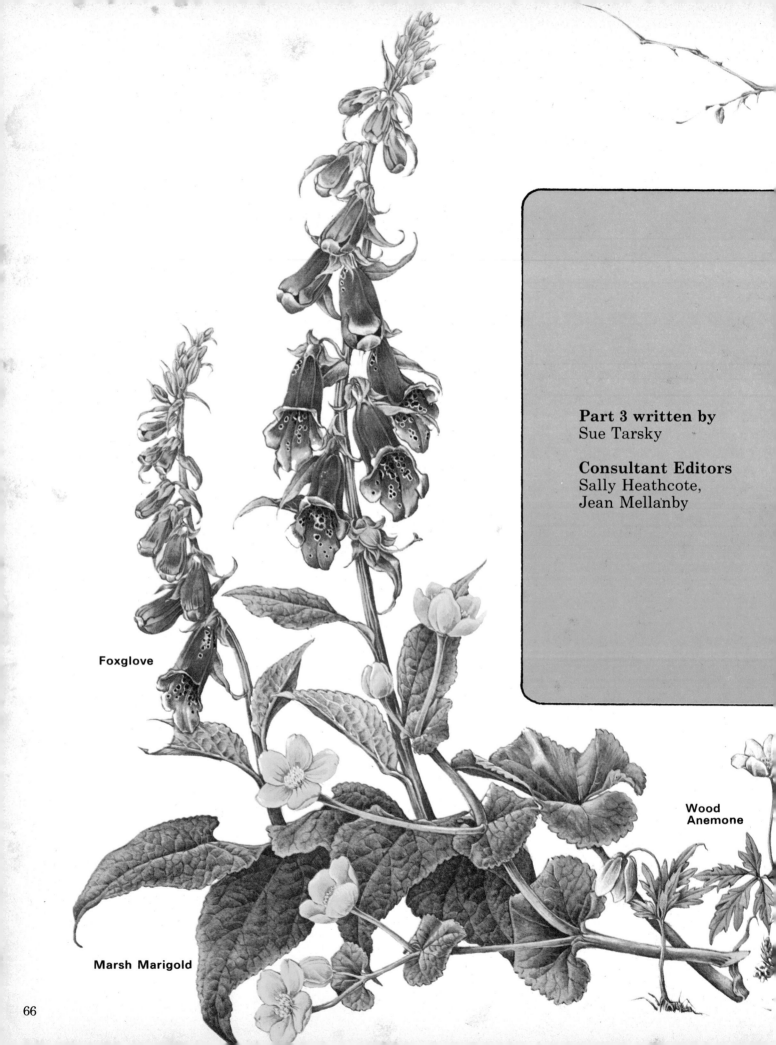

Foxglove

Part 3 written by
Sue Tarsky

Consultant Editors
Sally Heathcote,
Jean Mellanby

Wood
Anemone

Marsh Marigold

66

Part 3 WILD FLOWERS

Dog Rose

This section tells you where to look for common European wild flowers and how they live. There are several pages which tell you how to make field notes on flowers, and how to make a record book and a flower calendar.

Different species, or types, of wild flowers usually prefer particular kinds of places to live in. This section has lots of illustrations of these different habitats, and the

flowers that you can find in them. Often you will be able to find the flowers without having to go very far—even pavements and walls in towns can be good places for certain types of flowers.

Because so many of our wild flowers are dying out, a law has been passed in Britain to protect them. It is now illegal to dig up wild plants unless you have the permission of the landowner. So do not harm wild flowers

that you find—leave them for other people to see and enjoy. You can always record your find by making a drawing or photograph, and it is also interesting to come back to the same spot and study the flower as it changes through the seasons.

Herb Robert

Bluebell

Speedwell

Looking for Wild Flowers

When you go looking for wild flowers, take a notebook and two pencils with you for making quick sketches. Write down everything about a flower as soon as you see it. A magnifying glass is useful for looking at the small parts, and a tape measure for finding its height. Don't dig up flowers, and only pick them if you are sure they are common, and there are lots of the same kind growing together. Take sheets of newspaper to press the flowers. Use an outdoor thermometer to note the air temperature.

What You Need

Pencil

Notebook

Magnifying glass

Book with newspaper

Thermometer

Tape measure

July 12th 1975
Trent meadows. 20°C

flowers are yellow

flower heads are 20mm across

flowers are flat on top

flowers look like daisy

plant has hairs

leaves are oval and pointed at ends

leaves have wavy edges

plant is 40cm high

Magnifying glass

Petal

Stamens

Sepal

Stigma

Ovary

This is what the inside of a Buttercup looks like. Other flowers may look different. Try to draw what you see inside the flower you have found.

The three flowers shown on the right are very rare indeed. If you think you may have found a rare wild flower, do not pick it. If you do, it will die and be even more rare. Instead, draw the flower and show your drawing to an adult who knows about rare flowers.

If it is rare, you can report it to a conservation or nature club in your area. An expert may be able to gather some seeds when they fall from the flower and plant them carefully so that they will grow.

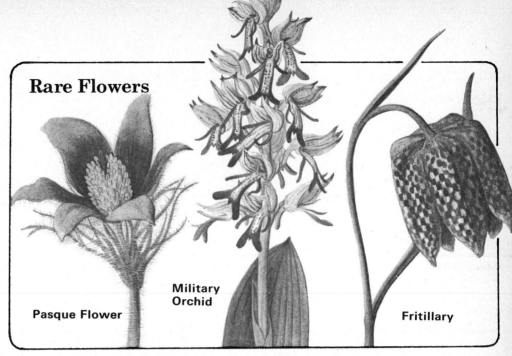

Rare Flowers

Pasque Flower

Military Orchid

Fritillary

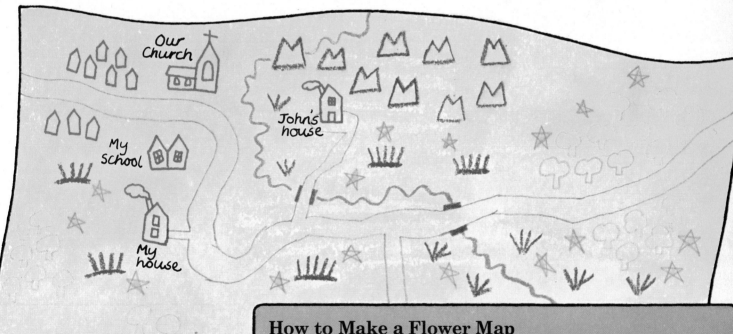

Our Church

John's house

My school

My house

50 paces

Symbols for your map

☆ FLOWERS
🍄 WOODS
∿ STREAM
🌾 GRASSLAND
⌂ HILLS
🌿 MARSHES, WATER
▬ BRIDGE
⌂⌂ HOUSES

How to Make a Flower Map

The easiest way to make a map is to draw it as you walk along a route you know well. Draw lines for the road or path and make it turn in the same way that you do. Put in symbols for bridges, buildings and other special places. Wherever you find a wild flower, mark the place on your map with a star.

Draw the symbols and write what they stand for on the bottom of your map so that everyone can understand them. If you like, you can use a scale to show distance so that anyone can follow your map. You can choose any scale you want. This map shows that 2 cm. is equal to 50 paces.

How Plants Live

The Rosebay Willowherb and the Field Buttercup have flowers with petals and sepals, and also leaves, stems and roots. Most other plants have the same parts, but they are often different shapes and sizes.

Each part of the plant does at least one special thing that helps the plant to live. The leaves make food for the plant. During the day, they take in carbon dioxide, a gas in the air, and together with the green colouring of the leaves, water and sunlight, make food. The leaves take in gases and give out gases and water through holes that are so small that you cannot see them, even with a magnifying glass.

The flower is a very important part of the plant. It is here that the seeds grow.

The petals may be brightly coloured or scented to attract insects. Some flowers need insects to carry pollen to other flowers for pollination (see page 72), so the brighter the colours, the more insects the flower will attract.

The sepals protect the flower when it is in bud. When the flower opens, they lie underneath the petals. All the sepals together are called the calyx.

The leaves make food and "breathe" for the plant. They also get rid of any water that the plant does not need. Because leaves need light to make food, the whole plant grows towards light. Some plants close their leaves at night.

The stem carries water from the roots to the leaves, and carries food made in the leaves to the rest of the plant. It also holds the leaves up to the light.

The roots hold the plant firmly in the ground, and take up water from the soil that the plant needs.

Rosebay Willowherb

Field Buttercup

How to Recognize Flowers

Colour

The easiest thing to notice first about a flower is its colour. A few examples are shown below. But you should also look at the shape of its petals, sepals and leaves.

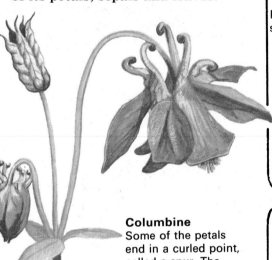

Columbine
Some of the petals end in a curled point, called a spur. The flower grows in woods and lowlands.

Bloody Cranesbill
The flowers are a bright purplish crimson and grow in dry, grassy places.

Bluebell
Bluebells are mostly blue, and sometimes white. They have a stalk with no leaves on it.

Petals

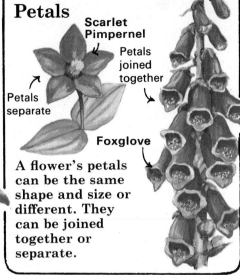

Scarlet Pimpernel — Petals joined together

Petals separate

Foxglove

A flower's petals can be the same shape and size or different. They can be joined together or separate.

Flowers and Stems

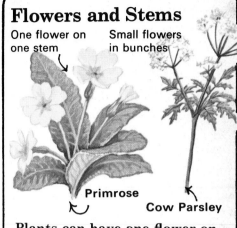

One flower on one stem — Small flowers in bunches

Primrose — Cow Parsley

Plants can have one flower on one stem, or many small flowers bunched together.

Sepals

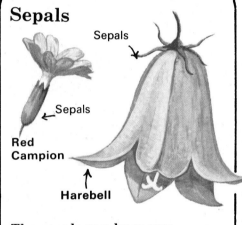

Sepals

Sepals

Red Campion

Harebell

The sepals can be many different shapes and sizes, joined together or separate.

Leaves

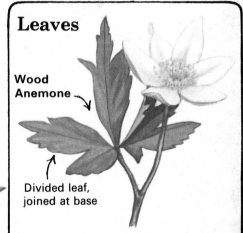

Wood Anemone

Divided leaf, joined at base

Leaves can be single, as in the Bugle, or divided into separate parts. In the Wood Anemone, the separate parts are joined together at the base. Sometimes the parts are on little stalks on a larger stalk. These are called leaflets.

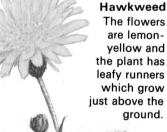

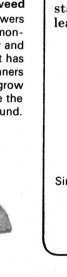

Mouse-ear Hawkweed
The flowers are lemon-yellow and the plant has leafy runners which grow just above the ground.

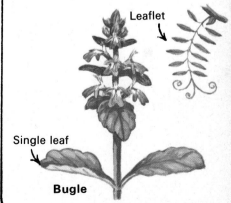

Leaflet

Single leaf

Bugle

How Flowers Grow

Almost every plant has a male part, called the stamen, and a female part, called the pistil. The Common Poppy has a group of stamens which grow around the pistil in the centre of the flower (see no. 3).

This page tells you how the stamens and the pistil in a Poppy together make seeds, which will later leave the plant and grow to form new plants. Not all plants make seeds in this way, but many do.

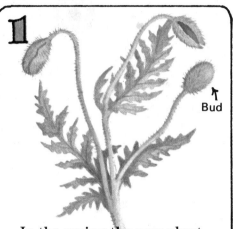

1

In the spring the new plant grows from a seed buried in the ground. There may be several flowers on one plant.

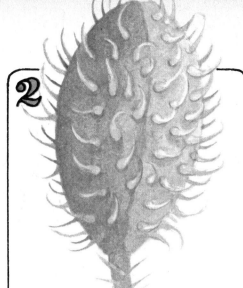

2

The sepals protect the flower when it is in bud. As the flower grows, the sepals begin to open.

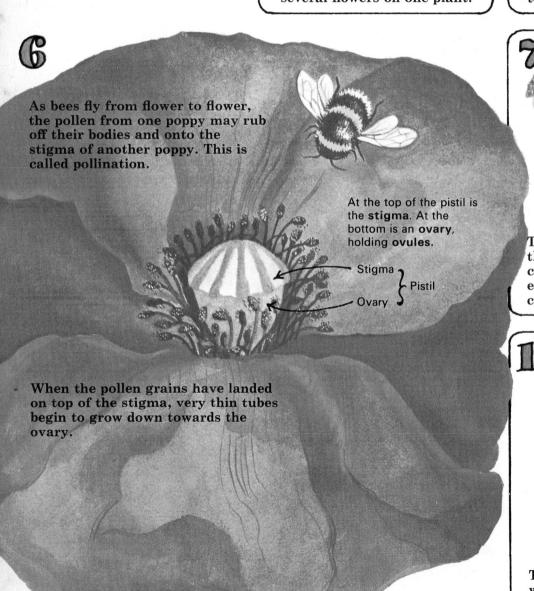

6

As bees fly from flower to flower, the pollen from one poppy may rub off their bodies and onto the stigma of another poppy. This is called pollination.

At the top of the pistil is the **stigma**. At the bottom is an **ovary**, holding **ovules**.

Stigma
Pistil
Ovary

When the pollen grains have landed on top of the stigma, very thin tubes begin to grow down towards the ovary.

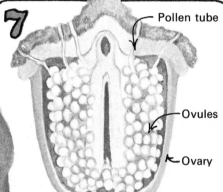

7

Pollen tube

Ovules

Ovary

The tubes eventually reach the ovules in the ovary. The contents of each pollen grain empty into an ovule. This is called fertilization.

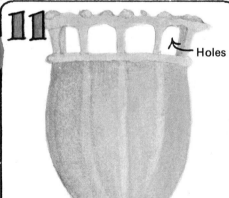

11

Holes

The fruit ripens. Its outside walls dry up and holes appear at the top.

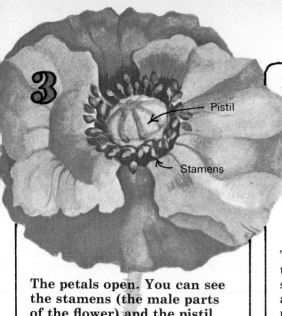

3 The petals open. You can see the stamens (the male parts of the flower) and the pistil (the female parts).

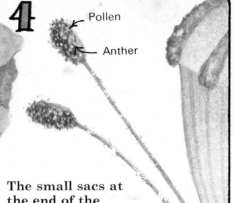

Pollen

Anther

4 The small sacs at the end of the stamens, called anthers, open. The yellow powder they hold, called pollen, escapes.

5 Bees visit the flower to feed. Pollen grains accidentally rub off on their hairy bodies or on their legs.

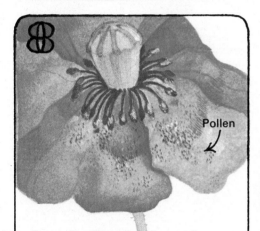

Pollen

8 Once fertilization has taken place, the pollen which is left is no longer needed, and it falls off.

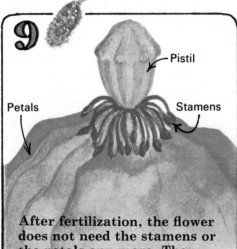

Pistil

Petals

Stamens

9 After fertilization, the flower does not need the stamens or the petals any more. They fall off. But the pistil is still needed. It remains strong.

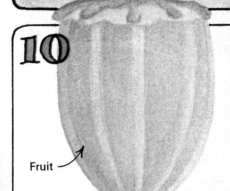

Fruit

10 Inside the pistil, the fertilized ovules are growing to form seeds. They are attached to the inside walls of the ovary. At this stage, the ovary is called the fruit.

The seeds which fall out of the fruit onto the soil in the autumn may grow into new plants the next spring.

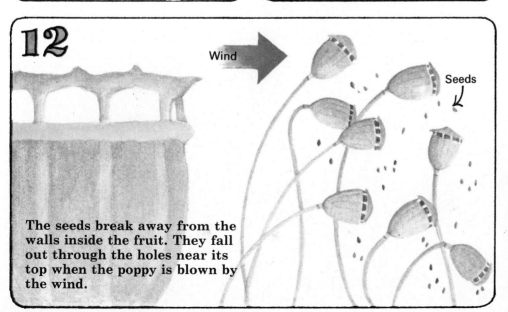

Wind

Seeds

12 The seeds break away from the walls inside the fruit. They fall out through the holes near its top when the poppy is blown by the wind.

How Pollen is Spread

In some plants, pollen from the stamens of one flower can make seeds grow in the ovary of the same flower. This is called self-pollination. In other plants, pollen must go from a flower of one plant to a flower of the same kind on a different plant. This is called cross-pollination. Pollen from a rose cannot make a seed grow in a daisy.

Most plants need insects to carry pollen, but some use the wind. Insects may go to a flower because of its scent or coloured petals. Some flowers have spots or lines on their petals called nectar guides. The insects follow these paths to find nectar.

Sometimes they must brush past the pollen, which sticks to their bodies. When they visit another flower, the pollen rubs off on the stigma.

Sometimes in summer the air is full of pollen, because the wind carries it from wind-pollinated flowers. It can make people sneeze, and give them hay-fever.

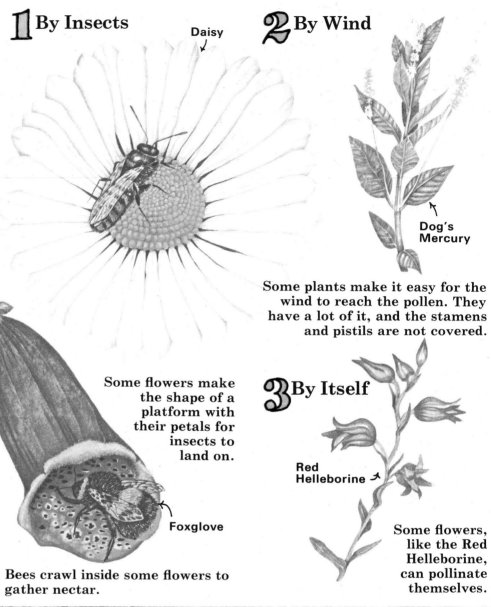

1 By Insects

Daisy

Some flowers make the shape of a platform with their petals for insects to land on.

Foxglove

Bees crawl inside some flowers to gather nectar.

2 By Wind

Dog's Mercury

Some plants make it easy for the wind to reach the pollen. They have a lot of it, and the stamens and pistils are not covered.

3 By Itself

Red Helleborine

Some flowers, like the Red Helleborine, can pollinate themselves.

What Plants Need

Wild flowers need to grow, spread their pollen, and make sure that their seeds are carried away from the parent plant. To do these things, they often depend on the weather, the soil and other living creatures—even people.

SOME PLANTS NEED INSECTS TO CARRY POLLEN

PLANTS NEED A BALANCE OF WATER AND MINERAL SALTS IN THE SOIL TO HELP THEM GROW AND FLOWER

PLANTS NEED CERTAIN TEMPERATURES, WHETHER THEY GROW IN COOL OR HOT PLACES. MOST EUROPEAN FLOWERS BLOOM WHEN IT IS WARM

PLANTS NEED LIGHT TO MAKE FOOD FOR THEMSELVES AND TO GROW

How Seeds are Scattered

Plants cannot produce seeds until they have been pollinated. Then they scatter seeds in different ways. Some use the wind, some use animals, some use water and some scatter their seeds themselves. They produce seeds that will be spread easily in at least one way. New plants need light to grow, so seeds grow best away from their parent plant, which might otherwise shadow them.

By Animals

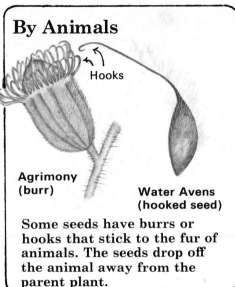

Agrimony (burr)

Hooks

Water Avens (hooked seed)

Some seeds have burrs or hooks that stick to the fur of animals. The seeds drop off the animal away from the parent plant.

By Wind

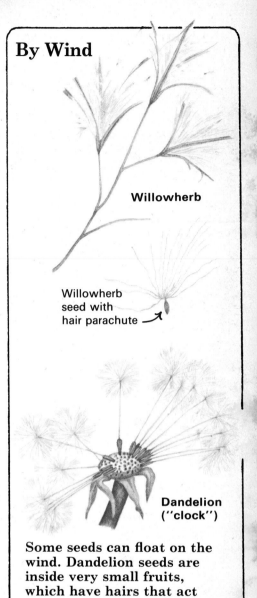

Willowherb

Willowherb seed with hair parachute

Dandelion ("clock")

Some seeds can float on the wind. Dandelion seeds are inside very small fruits, which have hairs that act like parachutes.

By Water

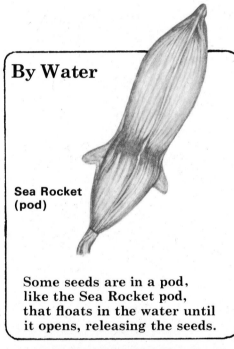

Sea Rocket (pod)

Some seeds are in a pod, like the Sea Rocket pod, that floats in the water until it opens, releasing the seeds.

By Explosion

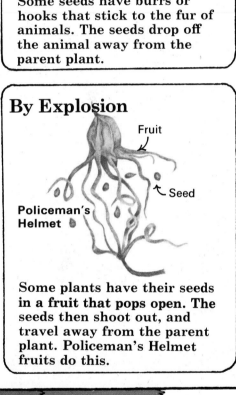

Fruit

Seed

Policeman's Helmet

Some plants have their seeds in a fruit that pops open. The seeds then shoot out, and travel away from the parent plant. Policeman's Helmet fruits do this.

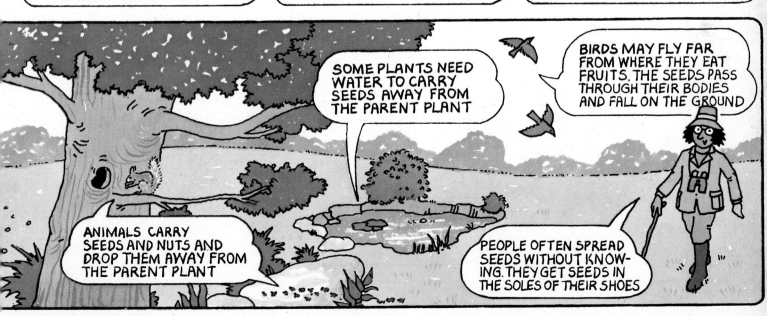

SOME PLANTS NEED WATER TO CARRY SEEDS AWAY FROM THE PARENT PLANT

BIRDS MAY FLY FAR FROM WHERE THEY EAT FRUITS. THE SEEDS PASS THROUGH THEIR BODIES AND FALL ON THE GROUND

ANIMALS CARRY SEEDS AND NUTS AND DROP THEM AWAY FROM THE PARENT PLANT

PEOPLE OFTEN SPREAD SEEDS WITHOUT KNOWING. THEY GET SEEDS IN THE SOLES OF THEIR SHOES

Flower Record Book

Keep a record book of everything you discover about wild flowers. If you use a loose-leaf binder, you can add pages whenever you wish. This is a perfect place to put any maps you have made, or even any photographs you have taken. Remember—anything to do with wild flowers belongs in your record book. Take down the results of your experiments in your book. Draw each step of an experiment as it happens. Write down what you see happening.

A Simple Experiment

Turn a plant away from the light. Come back a few days later. You will see that the plant is leaning towards the light. It is growing towards it because it needs light to make food.

1 Pressing and Mounting

If you pick a common flower you can press it. Put it between two sheets of blotting paper. Rest some heavy books on top.

2

When the flower is completely dry, put a dab of glue on the stem. Stick it carefully to the inside of a clear plastic bag, so you can see both sides.

3

If you find any flower heads on the ground, put them in the plastic bag, too. Stick the bag to a page in your book with sticky tape. Write the name of the flower if you know it and the date and place where you found it.

Common Mallow
Found in a grassy field on July 26th.

1 Leaf Printing

Put a leaf onto a flat surface with its underside facing you.

2

Cover it with a piece of thin white paper. Rub back and forth over the paper with a coloured crayon until the shape and veins show through.

3

Stick your leaf prints into your record book.

Common Fleabane
Found in a damp meadow on
August 8th.
at 11am
40cm high
21°C

Collecting Pictures

Stick magazine pictures or postcards of wild flowers into your book. This way you can see wild flowers even in the winter.

WRITE DOWN IN YOUR NOTEBOOK ANYTHING THAT YOU CAN FIND OUT ABOUT CUSTOMS OR FESTIVALS WHERE FLOWERS ARE USED

Drawing and Painting

Make detailed coloured drawings or paintings of the quick sketches you did in your notebook when you were outside. Be sure to write down the time of day when you saw the flowers, since plants may look different in the afternoon from in the morning.

Flower Calendar

You can see different flowers blooming in each season of the year. Make a calendar to help you remember them all. You can also see how a flower changes as the seasons change. Draw it once when it blooms and then draw it again a few months later.

The pictures of the Arum on the right show how different a flower can look at various stages in its life. (Two of the pictures show the inside of the flower.)

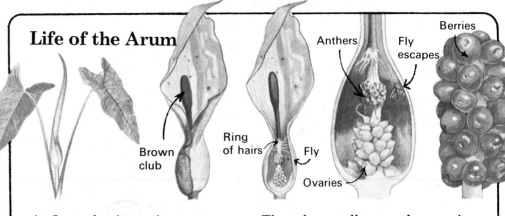

Life of the Arum

At first, the Arum is green. When the flower opens, it has a brown club. This attracts flies with its smell, and they get trapped inside by a ring of hairs.

They drop pollen on the ovaries. The hairs wither and the flies escape. In autumn, the ovaries develop into very poisonous red berries.

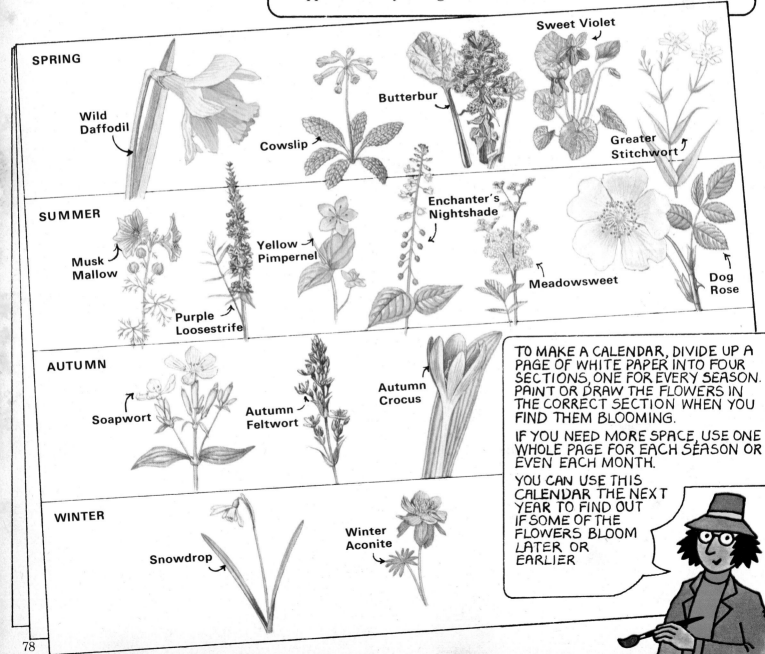

SPRING

Wild Daffodil

Cowslip

Butterbur

Sweet Violet

Greater Stitchwort

SUMMER

Musk Mallow

Purple Loosestrife

Yellow Pimpernel

Enchanter's Nightshade

Meadowsweet

Dog Rose

AUTUMN

Soapwort

Autumn Feltwort

Autumn Crocus

WINTER

Snowdrop

Winter Aconite

TO MAKE A CALENDAR, DIVIDE UP A PAGE OF WHITE PAPER INTO FOUR SECTIONS, ONE FOR EVERY SEASON. PAINT OR DRAW THE FLOWERS IN THE CORRECT SECTION WHEN YOU FIND THEM BLOOMING.

IF YOU NEED MORE SPACE, USE ONE WHOLE PAGE FOR EACH SEASON OR EVEN EACH MONTH.

YOU CAN USE THIS CALENDAR THE NEXT YEAR TO FIND OUT IF SOME OF THE FLOWERS BLOOM LATER OR EARLIER

Rivers and Ponds

Look for plants in different places near fresh water. If they grow in the water, they may be rooted to the bottom or have their roots floating. Their leaves may be under the water or floating on top of it. If plants are growing on the land, they may be at the water's edge, on the banks, or in swamps. Most water plants have their flowers above the surface of the water. They are usually pollinated by insects or wind, not by water.

Yellow Iris
The Yellow Iris has unusual petals and the leaves are very stiff and pointed. Look for stripes on the petals—they are nectar guides.

Frogbit
The Frogbit has shoots that grow sideways. New plants grow upwards from these shoots.

Duckweed
Duckweed can grow to cover a whole pond. It floats on top of still water.

Reedmace

Anthers

Seeds

The seeds of the Reedmace have silky parachutes that the wind carries. You can pick the flower for decoration, as this plant grows in large groups. Let them dry at home and then, if you wish, paint them.

Water Lily
The petals of the Water Lily give shade to pond creatures in hot weather. They can rest on the broad, thick leaves.

Policeman's Helmet
This flower has its seeds in a fruit. When the seeds are fully grown, the fruit explodes if anything touches it. You can collect these seeds in the late summer and plant them in the spring.

Pod

The Leaves of Water Plants
The leaves of plants growing in the water are of all shapes and sizes. They can be oval, round, short or long. This is because some grow under still water, some grow under fast-moving water and others grow on top of the water.

The Water Crowfoot has broad leaves above the water and thread-like leaves below the water.

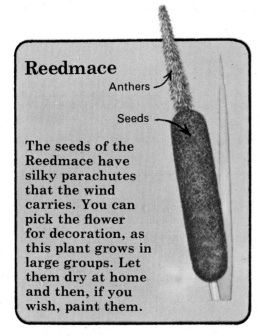

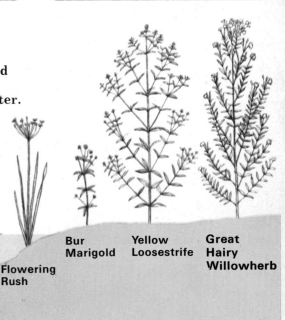

Spiked Water Milfoil

Water Soldier

Great Bladderwort

Water Crowfoot

Amphibious Bistort

Flowering Rush

Bur Marigold

Yellow Loosestrife

Great Hairy Willowherb

Fields, Meadows and Marshes

Fields vary from place to place and so do the flowers that grow in them. Fields can be used for pasturing animals or for growing crops. Meadows are used for growing hay, and marshes are grassy areas which are waterlogged all, or almost all, of the time.

You will find different flowers in different kinds of field, meadow or marsh, depending on what the area is used for, and how wet or dry the soil is. Wet soil is rich in many things that plants need, so you will usually find a lot of flowers.

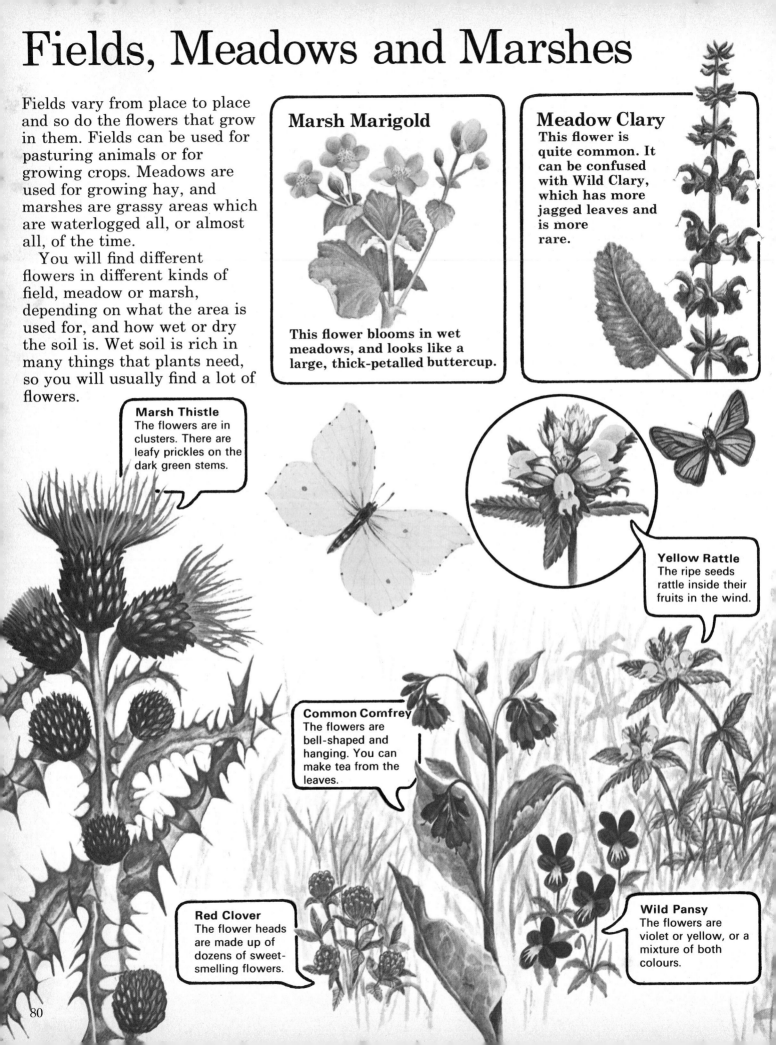

Marsh Marigold

This flower blooms in wet meadows, and looks like a large, thick-petalled buttercup.

Meadow Clary
This flower is quite common. It can be confused with Wild Clary, which has more jagged leaves and is more rare.

Marsh Thistle
The flowers are in clusters. There are leafy prickles on the dark green stems.

Yellow Rattle
The ripe seeds rattle inside their fruits in the wind.

Common Comfrey
The flowers are bell-shaped and hanging. You can make tea from the leaves.

Red Clover
The flower heads are made up of dozens of sweet-smelling flowers.

Wild Pansy
The flowers are violet or yellow, or a mixture of both colours.

Marsh Orchid
This plant has very unusual pink flowers. You should never pick it, or dig up the roots, as it is quite rare.

The flowers on this page can all be found in damp meadows. You will probably find different kinds of flowers in drier fields, and many of them are illustrated in the charts on pages 92–95. It is important to notice where flowers are growing when you find them.

Marsh Orchids, for example, will often be found in the shade of a tree. Note down as much as you can about the place where you found the flower—what was the soil like in the field? Was there a stream nearby? What was the field used for?

Fruit

Creeping Buttercup
This plant has creeping stems, which root easily.

Water Avens
The sepals and petals are both red, and the flowers hang in a nodding position. The fruits are easy to spot.

Meadowsweet
The flowers are in clusters, and smell sweet to attract insects.

Creeping Jenny
The flowers are bell-shaped and the creeping stems are matted on the ground.

Common Valerian
These red-pink flowers are common near water. They smell very unpleasant. The stem is quite stout.

Water Forget-me-Not
This plant grows near water. It is covered in soft hairs and the flower has a yellow centre.

Hedgerows and Roadsides

A hedgerow is a line of scrub or bushes planted by man, but often other bushes start to grow in between the planted ones. Hedgerows are important because many plants, animals and birds live in them. As fields are mown or ploughed up, living things look for shelter and food there. Many hedges have been destroyed, but people are now trying to save the ones that remain.

Hedges provide shade and shelter for flowers. Look for plants that have grown from seeds trapped in the hedge. They are blown there by the wind.

Flowers growing at the roadside must be tough and strong. They have car exhaust fumes blown at them and litter dumped on them. Only plants that have learned how to spread and grow survive.

Dog Rose
Birds eat the red fruits, called rose hips.

Wild Clematis
The fruits have long white hairs.

Cow Parsley
The flowers form a landing platform for insects.

Honeysuckle
The flowers are pollinated at night by moths.

Greater Burdock
The fruits of this plant stick to the fur of animals.

Stinging Nettl
There are stingir hairs around the edge of the leav The flowers are green.

Teasel
In winter, teasels are brown and brittle.

Foxglove
These flowers are very poisonous. Do not touch them.

Dandelion
The seeds form a feathery "clock", and float away when you blow them.

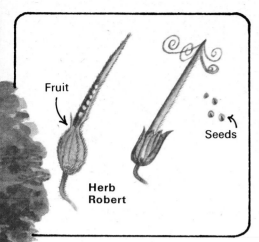

Look for the fruit of the Herb Robert. When the seeds are fully grown, the fruit explodes, and the seeds shoot out.

The Small Tortoiseshell butterfly lays its eggs on the leaves of the Stinging Nettle. If you find any eggs, do not touch them.

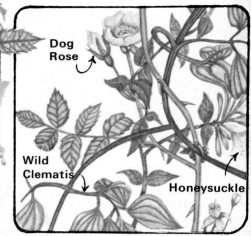

Wild Clematis and Honeysuckle twine themselves round the Dog Rose. It has backward-pointing thorns like hooks, to help it climb.

Make a Scent Jar

Make a scent jar from the petals of any flowers whose smell you like. The Dog Rose, Honeysuckle and Wild Strawberry are good flowers to use. You can put them in a jar or sew little bags from scraps of fabric. Be sure to leave one side of the bag open until you have put the dried petals inside.

Put the petals between two sheets of blotting paper and press them under a pile of books. With a pencil, punch holes in a circle of tin foil to

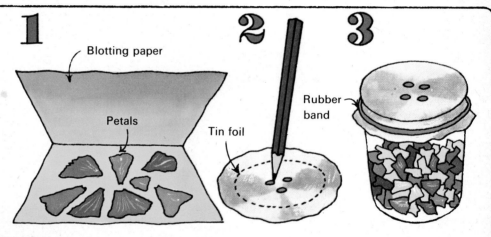

make the lid. When the petals are dry, put them in the jar with some pieces of dried

orange and lemon peel, and a bay leaf. Fix the foil lid over the jar with a rubber band.

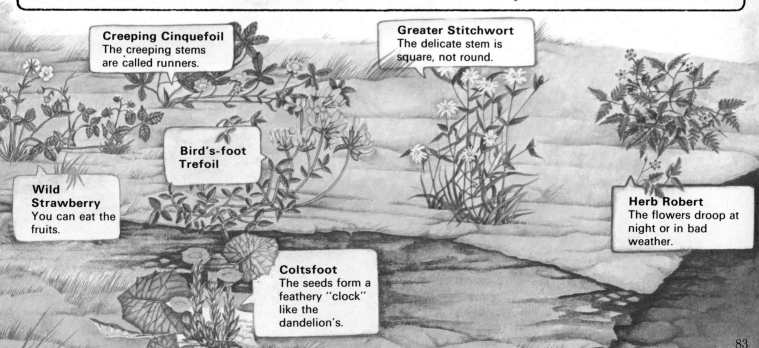

Creeping Cinquefoil The creeping stems are called runners.

Greater Stitchwort The delicate stem is square, not round.

Bird's-foot Trefoil

Wild Strawberry You can eat the fruits.

Herb Robert The flowers droop at night or in bad weather.

Coltsfoot The seeds form a feathery "clock" like the dandelion's.

Woodlands

When you see big and healthy trees in woods, you may find that there are not many flowers beneath them. The roots of the trees are probably taking almost all the food from the soil and their leaves are blocking the sunlight from reaching the flowers. Some wild flowers that grow in woods bloom in early spring. This is before the leaves on the trees are fully out. The kinds of flowers you will find change with the type of wood you are in and the seasons. Remember to look at the edge of woods. There is enough sunlight there for flowers to grow. See for yourself how many flowers grow near the edge and how many grow where it is very shady. How much of the ground in a wood is covered with flowers?

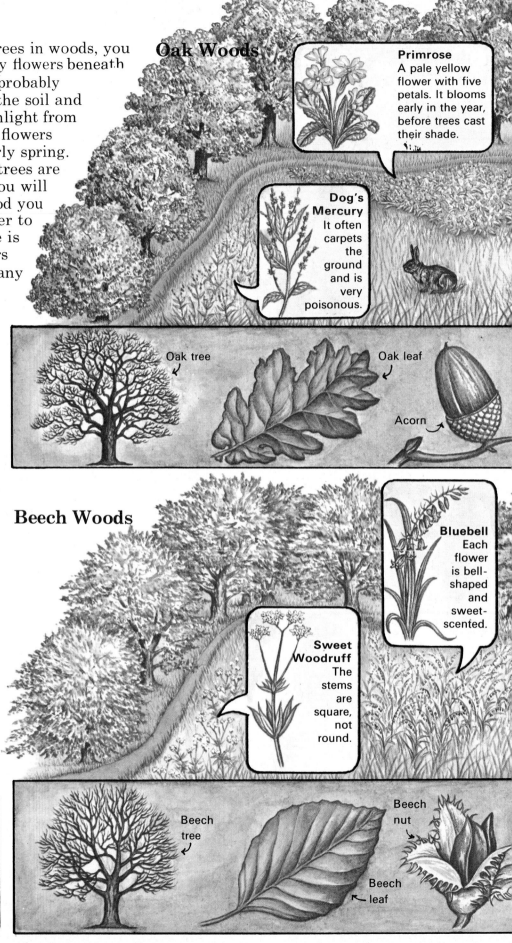

Oak Woods

Primrose
A pale yellow flower with five petals. It blooms early in the year, before trees cast their shade.

Dog's Mercury
It often carpets the ground and is very poisonous.

Oak tree

Oak leaf

Acorn

Beech Woods

Bluebell
Each flower is bell-shaped and sweet-scented.

Sweet Woodruff
The stems are square, not round.

Beech tree

Beech leaf

Beech nut

OAK WOODS
OAK TREES MAY GROW TO BE VERY LARGE. IF THEY DO, VERY LITTLE LIGHT FILTERS DOWN BENEATH THEIR LEAVES. EVEN THE GRASSES NEARBY WOULD NOT GROW VERY HIGH. A GOOD PLACE TO SEARCH FOR FLOWERS IN AN OAK WOOD IS NEAR PATHS AT THE EDGE OF THE WOOD

BEECH WOODS
BEECH TREES GROW BEST WHERE THE SOIL DOES NOT HOLD MUCH WATER. THE FLOWERS YOU WILL FIND IN A BEECH WOOD ALSO PREFER SOIL THAT IS NOT TOO WET. SEE IF THE FLOWERS YOU FIND IN A BEECH WOOD ARE DIFFERENT FROM THOSE IN AN OAK WOOD

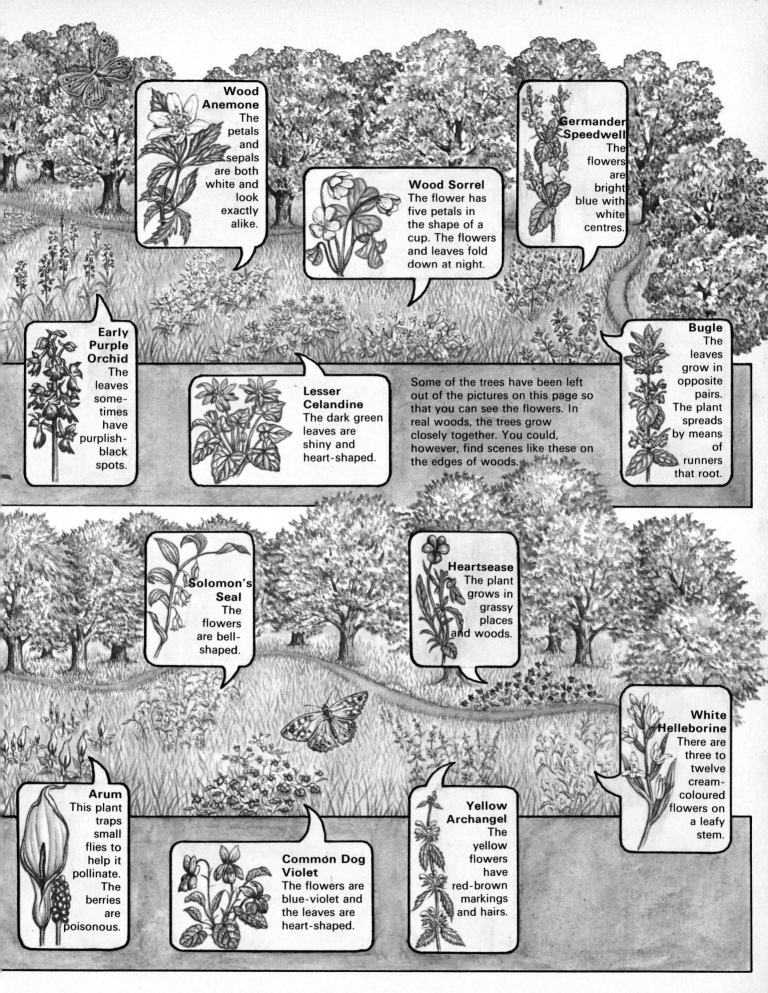

Wood Anemone The petals and sepals are both white and look exactly alike.

Wood Sorrel The flower has five petals in the shape of a cup. The flowers and leaves fold down at night.

Germander Speedwell The flowers are bright blue with white centres.

Early Purple Orchid The leaves sometimes have purplish-black spots.

Lesser Celandine The dark green leaves are shiny and heart-shaped.

Some of the trees have been left out of the pictures on this page so that you can see the flowers. In real woods, the trees grow closely together. You could, however, find scenes like these on the edges of woods.

Bugle The leaves grow in opposite pairs. The plant spreads by means of runners that root.

Solomon's Seal The flowers are bell-shaped.

Heartsease The plant grows in grassy places and woods.

White Helleborine There are three to twelve cream-coloured flowers on a leafy stem.

Arum This plant traps small flies to help it pollinate. The berries are poisonous.

Common Dog Violet The flowers are blue-violet and the leaves are heart-shaped.

Yellow Archangel The yellow flowers have red-brown markings and hairs.

85

The Seashore

Plants near the sea must learn how to survive. They must find ways to get water and then stop it escaping. To do this, some plants grow a thick outer layer to trap the water, while others have a waxy coat over their leaves, or roll up their leaves when it is very hot and sunny.

Some plants have hairs on their leaves which shield them from the sun and other plants have very small leaves, or grow spines instead of leaves, so that water cannot escape.

Plants must be sturdy enough not to blow over in strong winds. They may have deep roots to grip the mud or stones. The roots also take up water.

Salt Marshes

Salt-Marshes are made of sand and mud. Be careful when you walk there. It is very easy to sink in. Go with a friend and wear rubber boots. The land in such places has slowly taken over from the sea. That is why the soil is salty.

There are different zones in marshes. Different plants grow in each zone. You will probably not find the plants that grow in marshes further inland.

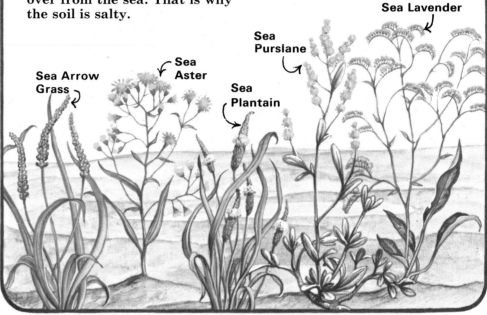

Sea Arrow Grass · Sea Aster · Sea Plantain · Sea Purslane · Sea Lavender

Sand Dunes

There are also different zones of sand dunes. They vary according to how far they are from the sea, and how much they have been built up or "fixed" by the growth of marram grass or other plants.

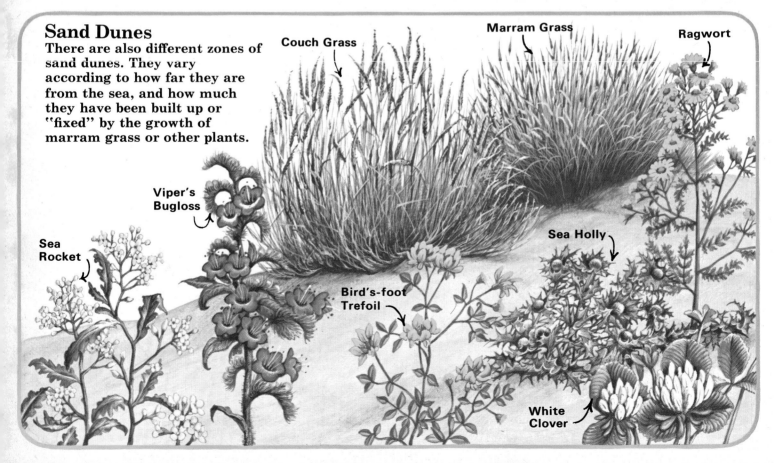

Couch Grass · Marram Grass · Ragwort · Viper's Bugloss · Sea Rocket · Bird's-foot Trefoil · Sea Holly · White Clover

Shingle Beaches

Not many plants can grow here. These beaches are made of pebbles that once were part of cliffs or rocks. They have been worn down by the pounding of the sea. There is some sand mixed in with the pebbles, but in many places they are constantly shifting. Plants like the Yellow Horned Poppy and the Sea Pea have deep roots that give them some anchorage in the shingle.

Shrubby Seablite

Sea Pea

Sea Bindweed

Yellow Horned Poppy

Cliffs

Plants must struggle to grow here. The wind blows almost all the time and tears up small plants whose roots are not deep. The water drains away quickly, leaving little for the plants and there is almost no soil. The plants must send their roots deep into cracks in the rock.

They sometimes grow along the steep angles of the cliff and are often sprayed with salty water from the sea. Sometimes cliffs have some soil towards the top where you will be able to find land plants.

Be careful when you look at flowers here. Do not climb any cliffs, and keep well back from the edge.

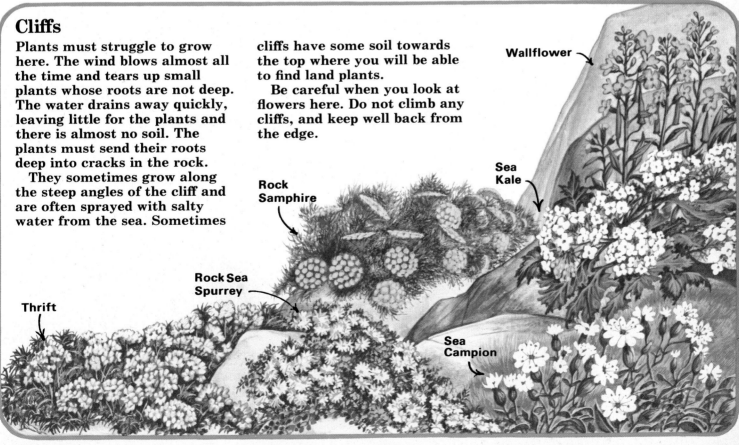

Wallflower

Sea Kale

Rock Samphire

Rock Sea Spurrey

Thrift

Sea Campion

Towns

Flowers grow in waste lands, walls, streets, car parks, gardens, churchyards or any other places in towns where they can find enough soil. Many flowers have learned how to spread in open ground. Some of these flowers are called weeds. Weeds are a problem to people growing other plants, because they take over the land. Many of the seeds of weed plants are spread by the wind, and some by water.

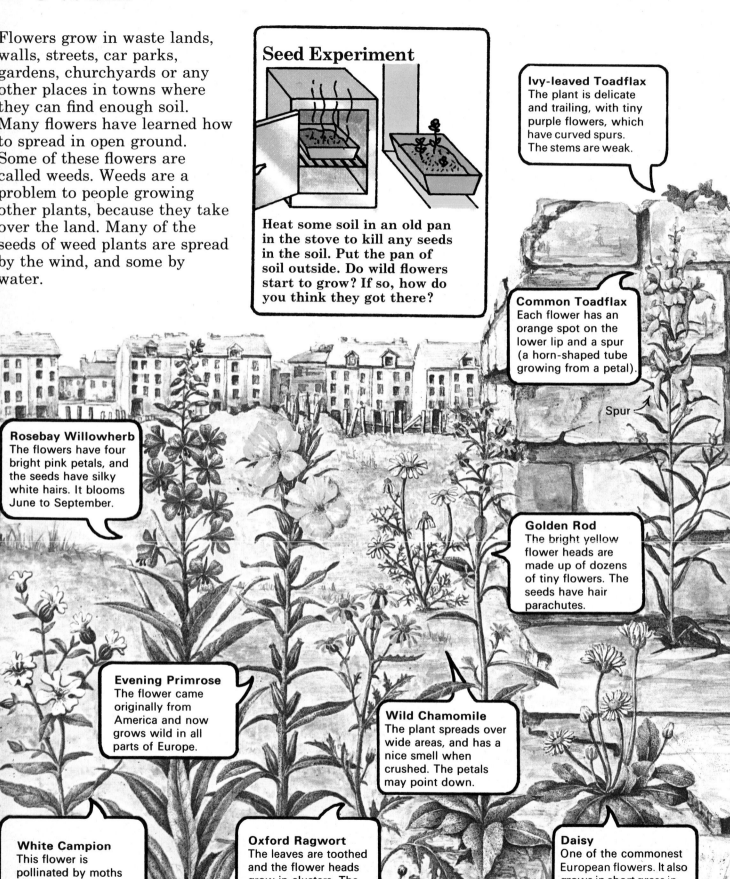

Seed Experiment

Heat some soil in an old pan in the stove to kill any seeds in the soil. Put the pan of soil outside. Do wild flowers start to grow? If so, how do you think they got there?

Ivy-leaved Toadflax
The plant is delicate and trailing, with tiny purple flowers, which have curved spurs. The stems are weak.

Common Toadflax
Each flower has an orange spot on the lower lip and a spur (a horn-shaped tube growing from a petal).

Spur

Rosebay Willowherb
The flowers have four bright pink petals, and the seeds have silky white hairs. It blooms June to September.

Golden Rod
The bright yellow flower heads are made up of dozens of tiny flowers. The seeds have hair parachutes.

Evening Primrose
The flower came originally from America and now grows wild in all parts of Europe.

Wild Chamomile
The plant spreads over wide areas, and has a nice smell when crushed. The petals may point down.

White Campion
This flower is pollinated by moths at night, and the plant has sticky hairs on it.

Oxford Ragwort
The leaves are toothed and the flower heads grow in clusters. The plant grows on bare or waste ground.

Daisy
One of the commonest European flowers. It also grows in short grass in fields. The flowers close up at night.

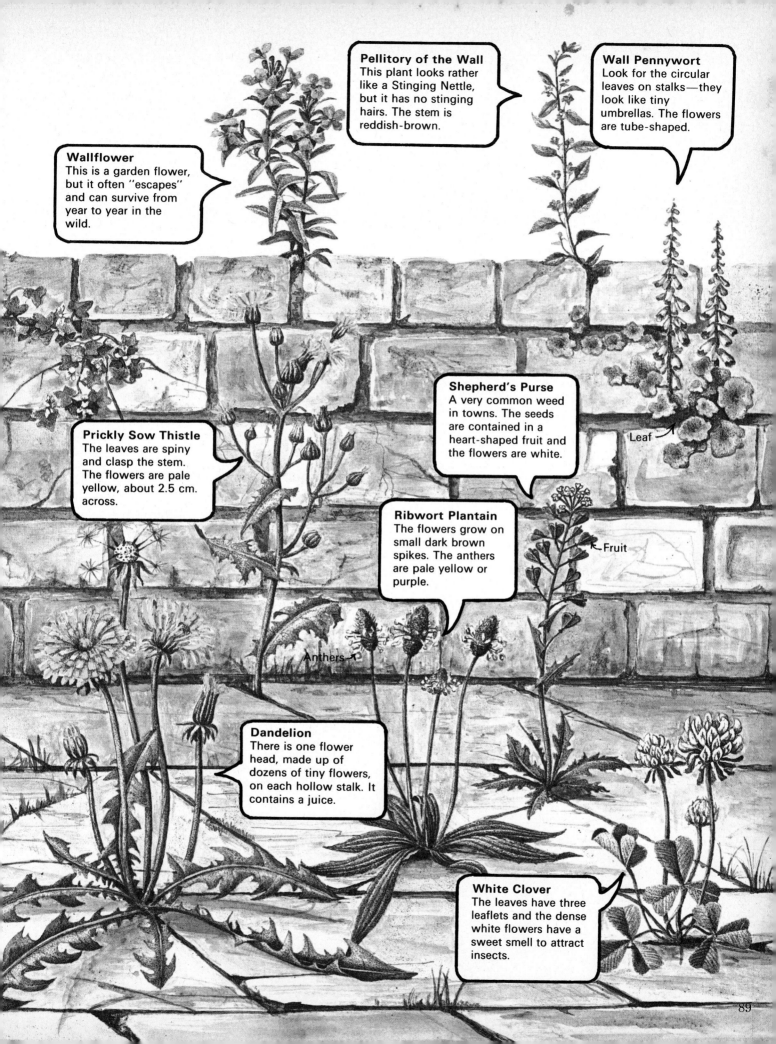

Moors and Mountains

Moors

There are fewer wild flowers that you will find growing on heaths and moors than in fields or meadows. The ones that are able to grow sometimes take over large areas of moorland.

Both heaths and moors are open lands that are swept by wind. Some are very dry and some are waterlogged from time to time. Water collects where the soil is very poor, such as in high land, or areas near the coast.

Different flowers grow on different types of moorland and heath. The most common plant of moorland is heather. It is sometimes burnt to encourage new shoots to grow.

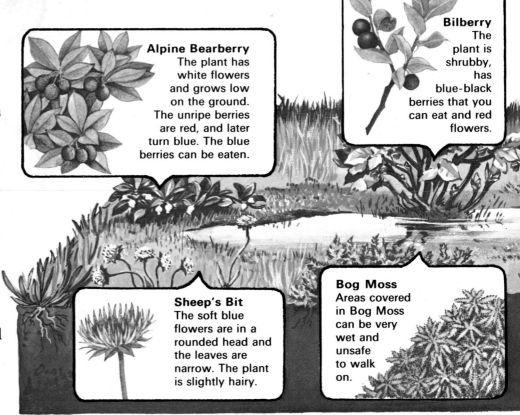

Alpine Bearberry
The plant has white flowers and grows low on the ground. The unripe berries are red, and later turn blue. The blue berries can be eaten.

Bilberry
The plant is shrubby, has blue-black berries that you can eat and red flowers.

Sheep's Bit
The soft blue flowers are in a rounded head and the leaves are narrow. The plant is slightly hairy.

Bog Moss
Areas covered in Bog Moss can be very wet and unsafe to walk on.

Mountains

The seeds of mountain flowers find it difficult to grow in the poor soils and cold, windy weather of mountain-sides. The higher up a mountain you go, the fewer flowers you will find growing. Trees cannot grow high up on mountains because of the strong winds and lack of soil.

Some plants, however, can grow high up the mountain-side. They are low ones that will not be blown away by high winds. Many flowers that grow on mountains spread by sending out creeping runner shoots which root.

Common Heather (Ling)
The plant usually takes over the area in which it grows. Its leaves are in opposite pairs and the flowers are pale purple. The plant also grows on moors and heaths and blooms in August.

Alpine Fleabane
The flowers have yellow centres with pale purple rays around them. The plant is short and hairy.

Common Butterwort
The leaves are broad and their edges roll up to trap and digest insects.

Sundew
The rounded red leaves are covered with long sticky hairs that trap insects and digest them.

Bell Heather
A very common flower on heaths and moors, with needle-like leaves that grow in threes.

Starry Saxifrage
The leaves are fleshy and shiny. The tiny white flowers have pink anthers.

Harebell
The petals of the flower are joined together to form a bell shape. The flowers hang in loose clusters on long, thin stalks.

Opposite-Leaved Golden Saxifrage
The leaves grow in opposite pairs on a square stem. The plant grows low on the ground.

Alpine Lady's Mantle
The leaves have silvery-grey hairs on their undersides.

Moss Campion
The leaves are tiny and pointed, and there are usually many flowers growing together, forming a dense mat on the ground.

Alpine Forget-me-Not
The plant has small blue flowers, and the leaves are soft and downy. The sepals are covered in silvery hairs.

Alpine Milk Vetch
The leaves have four to eight pairs of leaflets, and the flowers are lilac and white, often with purple tips.

Other Common Flowers to Spot

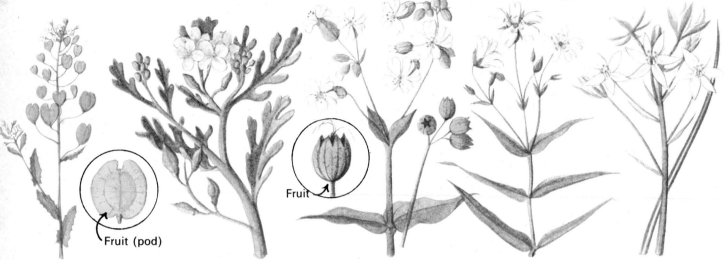

Field Pennycress
30 cm. Waste ground.
Summer.

Fruit (pod)

Sea Rocket
30 cm. Sandy coasts.
Summer.

Fruit

Bladder Campion
45 cm. Waste ground,
grassy places.
Spring/Summer.

Greater Stitchwort
20 cm. Woods, hedges,
fields. Spring.

Star-of-Bethlehem
15 cm. Grassy places.
Early Summer.

Cloudberry
15 cm. Upland bogs,
damp moors.
Summer.

White Stonecrop
Low and creeping.
Rocks, walls.
Summer.

White Bryony
Climbing to 4 m.
Hedges, scrub.
Spring/Summer.

White Dead Nettle
20 cm. Waysides,
waste places.
Spring to Autumn.

Feverfew
30 cm. Walls,
waste places.
Summer.

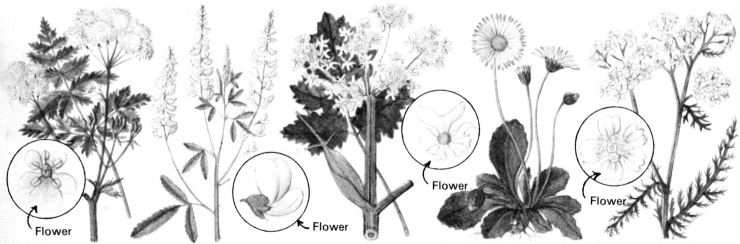

Flower

Flower

Flower

Flower

Cow Parsley
60 cm. Hedge-banks,
shady places.
Spring.

White Melilot
60 cm. Bare and
waste ground.
Summer.

Hogweed
Up to 3 m. Grassy
places, open woods.
Spring to Autumn.

Daisy
10 cm. Lawns,
short turf, fields.
All year.

Yarrow
30 cm.
Grassy places.
Summer/Autumn.

92 Remember—if you cannot see a picture of the flower you want to identify here, look on the page earlier in the book which deals with the kind of place where you found it.

The figure given in metres or centimetres is the average height of the flower from ground level to the top of the plant. The season given is when the plant is in flower. The captions also give the kind of place where the flower is most commonly found.

Bulbous Buttercup
15 cm. Grassland.
Spring.

Marsh Marigold
15 cm.
Wet places.
Spring/Summer.

Yellow Horned Poppy
60 cm. Sea shingle,
waste places inland.
Summer.

Monkey Flower
20 cm.
Wet places.
Summer.

Yellow Rattle
30 cm. Grassy places,
cornfields.
Spring/Summer.

Wild Cabbage
60 cm.
Sea cliffs.
Summer.

Silverweed
Creeping with runners.
Damp, grassy places.
Spring/Summer.

Lady's Bedstraw
10 cm. Dry,
grassy places.
Summer.

Yellow Chamomile
30 cm. Dry, bare
and waste places.
Summer.

Groundsel
10 cm. Weed found in
gardens and on waste
ground. All year.

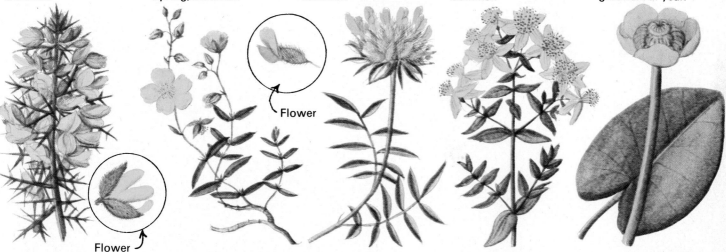

Common Gorse
Grows up to 2½ m.
Heaths, grassland.
All year.

Common Rockrose
Close to the ground.
Grassy and rocky places.
Summer.

Kidney Vetch
15 cm. Dry grassland.
by sea, on mountains.
Spring/Summer.

**Perforate St.
John's Wort**
45 cm. Grassy and
bushy places. Summer.

Yellow Waterlily
A few cms. above water.
Still water, slow streams.
Summer.

Remember—if you cannot see a picture of the flower you want to identify here, look on the page earlier in the book which deals with the kind of place where you found it.

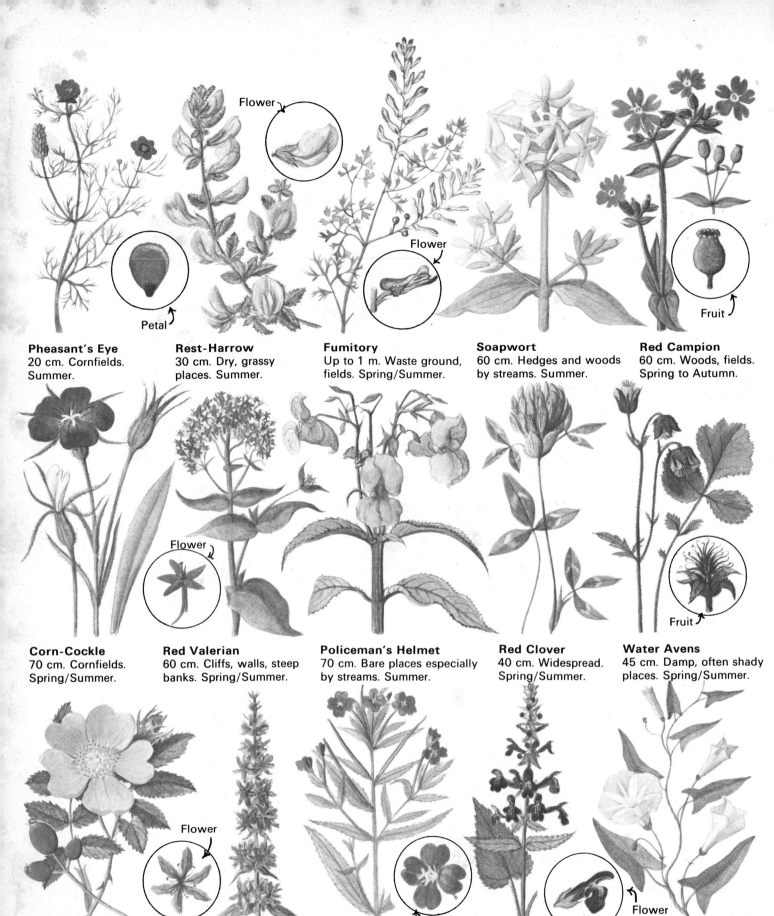

Pheasant's Eye
20 cm. Cornfields.
Summer.

Petal

Rest-Harrow
30 cm. Dry, grassy
places. Summer.

Flower

Fumitory
Up to 1 m. Waste ground,
fields. Spring/Summer.

Flower

Soapwort
60 cm. Hedges and woods
by streams. Summer.

Red Campion
60 cm. Woods, fields.
Spring to Autumn.

Fruit

Corn-Cockle
70 cm. Cornfields.
Spring/Summer.

Flower

Red Valerian
60 cm. Cliffs, walls, steep
banks. Spring/Summer.

Policeman's Helmet
70 cm. Bare places especially
by streams. Summer.

Red Clover
40 cm. Widespread.
Spring/Summer.

Water Avens
45 cm. Damp, often shady
places. Spring/Summer.

Fruit

Dog Rose
Grows up to 3 m.
Hedges and scrub.
Early Summer.

Flower

Purple Loosestrife
70 cm. Damp places
especially by rivers.
Summer.

Great Hairy Willowherb
70 cm. Damp places,
Summer.

Flower

Hedge Woundwort
45 cm. Hedge-banks,
shady places. Summer.

Flower

Field Bindweed
Climbing to 2 m.
Weed found on waste
ground. Summer.

94   **Remember—if you cannot see a picture of the flower you want to identify here, look on the page earlier
in the book which deals with the kind of place where you found it.**

Some flowers are more widespread in some localities than others—you may be able to find several of one type growing in one area, and none at all in another.

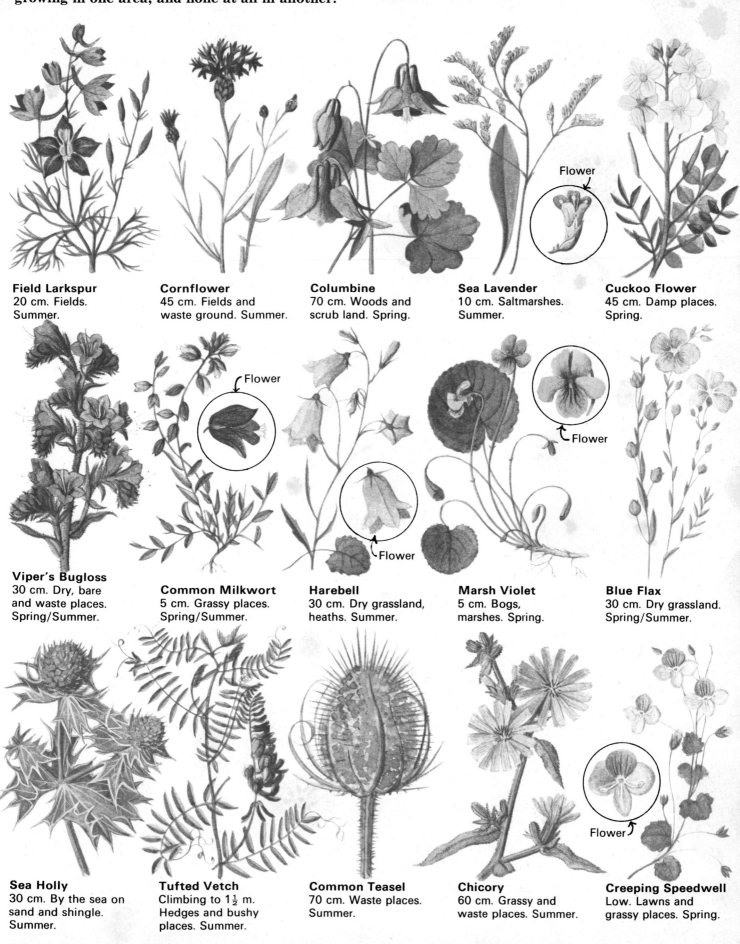

Field Larkspur
20 cm. Fields.
Summer.

Cornflower
45 cm. Fields and
waste ground. Summer.

Columbine
70 cm. Woods and
scrub land. Spring.

Sea Lavender
10 cm. Saltmarshes.
Summer.

Flower

Cuckoo Flower
45 cm. Damp places.
Spring.

Flower

Flower

Flower

Flower

Viper's Bugloss
30 cm. Dry, bare
and waste places.
Spring/Summer.

Common Milkwort
5 cm. Grassy places.
Spring/Summer.

Harebell
30 cm. Dry grassland,
heaths. Summer.

Marsh Violet
5 cm. Bogs,
marshes. Spring.

Blue Flax
30 cm. Dry grassland.
Spring/Summer.

Flower

Sea Holly
30 cm. By the sea on
sand and shingle.
Summer.

Tufted Vetch
Climbing to 1½ m.
Hedges and bushy
places. Summer.

Common Teasel
70 cm. Waste places.
Summer.

Chicory
60 cm. Grassy and
waste places. Summer.

Creeping Speedwell
Low. Lawns and
grassy places. Spring.

Remember—if you cannot see a picture of the flower you want to identify here, look on the page earlier in the book which deals with the kind of place where you found it.

Book List

A Field Guide to the Birds of Britain and Europe. R. T. Peterson, G. Mountford and P. A. D. Hollom (Collins)
The Oxford Book of Birds and the *Pocket Oxford Book of Birds.* Bruce Campbell (Oxford)
The Wild Flowers of Britain and N. Europe. R. Fitter, A. Fitter, M. Blamey (Collins)
The Concise Flowers of Europe. O. Polunin (Oxford)
Know Your Broadleaves. H. L. Edlin (H.M.S.O.)
Know Your Conifers. H. L. Edlin (H.M.S.O.)
A Field Guide to the Trees of Britain and N. Europe. Alan Mitchell (Collins)
The NatureTrail Books—Insect-watching. Ruth Thomson; *Seashore Life.* Su Swallow; *Ponds and Streams.* Su Swallow (Usborne)
How Birds Live. Tony Bremner (Usborne)

For information on how to do a tree survey, write to: **The Council for the Protection of Rural England,** 4, Hobart Place, London SW1W 0HY.

Clubs and Societies

The national club for young birdwatchers is the **Young Ornithologists' Club.** Members receive their own magazine *Bird Life* every other month and may take part in competitions, projects and local outings. The Club also organizes birdwatching holidays in many parts of Britain. The YOC is the junior section of the **Royal Society for the Protection of Birds** and further details may be obtained from The Lodge, Sandy, Bedfordshire, SG19 2DL.
The British Trust for Ornithology organizes national surveys which are carried out by volunteers, and administers the ringing of birds. Junior members must be aged 15. Headquarters: Beech Grove, Tring, Hertfordshire.
The Wildfowl Trust owns several reserves for wildfowl and carries out important research. Junior members should join the **Gosling Club** and have free access to the Trust's collection and receive bulletins. Details from The New Grounds, Slimbridge, Gloucestershire.

The Wildlife Youth Service (address: Marston Court, 98–106 Manor Road, Wallington, Surrey) is a branch of the World Wildlife Fund.
The Botanical Society of the British Isles, c/o Natural History Museum, Cromwell Road, London SW7.
The Biological Records Centre at Monks Wood Experimental Station, Abbots Ripton, Huntingdon, co-ordinates survey work of people throughout Britain, to make records of changes in the countryside.
The Council for Nature (address: The Zoological Gardens, Regent's Park, London NW1 4RY) is a representative body of more than 450 societies, and will supply the addresses of your local **Natural History Societies.** (Send a stamped addressed envelope for list.) The Council will also give you the address of your local **County Naturalist Trust,** which may have a junior branch. Many of the Trusts have meetings, lectures, and opportunities for work on nature reserves.

Index